DESIGNED BY SCARLETT CREECH

This book is dedicated to
LILLIEBELL LOMBARDO
who was Guy's sweet inspiration
behind "The Sweetest Music
This Side of Heaven."

CONTENTS

Foreword By Lawrence Welk

Lawrence Welk recalls, "Like millions of American music lovers, I first became acquainted with Guy Lombardo and his Royal Canadians through the medium of radio in the 1920s. They were doing "remote" broadcasts from a club in Chicago, and I was a struggling young bandleader ('America's Biggest Little Band'), working out of Yankton, South Dakota. The first time I heard the Guy Lombardo Orchestra on the air, I remarked to my boys, 'That's the finest band I've ever heard.' I've been a Lombardo fan ever since, also an imitator to some degree. I'm not ashamed to admit that over the years I've borrowed the best features of some of the top name bands. In the Lombardo band, the features which particularly struck me were the distinctive sound of the saxophone section; the cleanness of the ensemble playing, the faithful adherence to the melody; the uncomplicated, understandable arrangements; and the fact that everything they played was pleasant to listen to and easy to dance to.

"Some years later, our band was working in the New York area at the time Guy was holding forth at the Roosevelt Hotel. Naturally I made it a point to drop in at the Roosevelt Grill and hear my idol in person. But I was too shy to introduce myself to Guy. After all, he was not only *my* idol, but the musical hero of millions as the leader of the most popular band in the country. Besides, I seriously doubted that the name Lawrence Welk would mean anything to a man of such stature in our business.

"In 1947 I had one of my greatest thrills when our band was hired for a short engagement at the very same Roosevelt Grill. I'm afraid our success at the prestigious establishment didn't quite measure up to that of our famous predecessor. I guess our band wasn't ready for New York (or maybe New York wasn't ready for Lawrence Welk!). One episode in particular ranks among my all-time favorite 'Bubble Busters'. One evening a rather haughty lady, obviously a member of New York Cafe Society, complete with Paris gown, diamond jewelry and lorgnette, approached me and asked, 'Is this the Guy Lombardo orchestra?' Turning on my best Strasburg, North Dakota, charm, I told her, 'No Ma'am, this is the Champagne Music of Lawrence Welk.' Perhaps my accent was too much for her, because I had to repeat my answer. Her reaction didn't exactly bolster my ego. Giving me a withering look through her lorgnette, she said, 'Well, it stinks!' The language may not have been pure "Park Avenue," but the meaning was unmistakable. I was sorely tempted to return to the farm, the plow, the overalls, and the barn.

"Guy and I became close friends many years ago. One of my treasured memories is the Eisenhower Inaugural Ball of 1957, at which both of our bands had the honor of playing. We enjoyed some pleasant moments of reminiscing when our two bands shared a charter flight from Washington to Newark, New Jersey, following the inaugural.

"We also shared the frightening experience of a near-crash landing at the Newark airport. Guy exhibited exceptional poise as well as a little-known sense of humor at the height of danger. Turning to me, he very casually remarked, 'Lawrence, if this crate happens to crash, you know that tomorrow morning Sammy Kaye will have the top commercial band in America.'

"In our early years we often had trouble securing bookings. Tom Archer, who owned many ballrooms in the Midwest, was able to hire the best of the name bands for five hundred dollars a night. We were classified as a 'Territory Band,' with a reputation extending over only a limited area, so we could hardly cope with this kind of competition. I *do* know that for several years Tom had a standing offer to Guy for *fifteen hundred dollars* a night. To the best of my knowledge, he was never able to secure the services of the Lombardo band even at that unheard-of price. (Remember, these were pre-inflation days.) Incidentally, Tom and I later became close friends and our band played many of Tom's ballrooms over the years.

"Yes, I have some fond memories of Guy and his wonderful band, deep appreciation for what he did for our music business, and much gratitude in my heart for his personal friendship. On at least one of our TV shows each year, we pay tribute to some of the great name bands, and we never fail to include my personal favorite, Guy Lombardo.

"I'm only sorry that I must miss his traditional New Year's Eve Party. It seems that after fifty-three years in this business, I just wouldn't feel right not being on the bandstand myself (usually the Hollywood Palladium), helping the dancers enjoy themselves, and above all, precisely at midnight, playing the song so long identified with a great man and a great band—'Auld Lang Syne.' To paraphrase this famous theme, Should auld acquaintance be forgot, I'm sure America will never forget Guy Lombardo and his Royal Canadians."

Guy and Lawrence Welk munch on a Squeezeburger, an early 1930 Welk Enterprise that ended in failure.

Both bandleaders check on their so-called squareness at Rainbow Grill in N.Y.C. during an engagement by the Royal Canadians in 1968.

Lawrence Welk dances to the music of the Lombardo band at the Rainbow Grill.

The Legacy

Author's Note:

Guy Lombardo was taken for granted, like the Statue of Liberty, Niagara Falls and New Year's Eve. For millions of dancers throughout the United States and Canada, he became an institution, a way of life, and a national pastime. He and his orchestra represented an unfaded memento from an opulent past that towered above the confusion of the present like a monument that was itself greater than the ideal it commemorated. Guy neither lived in the past, nor did he try to reconstruct it. As the circle of time completes its evolution, values of yesterday, like antiques and heirlooms, are enriched, not destroyed; recognized and treasured.

The Lombardo charisma was both simple and complex. Over the years he created an image with which he lived with an unbending loyalty. The maestro was a charming, gracious gentleman. His low-key showmanship manifested itself in a smile and a friendly nod. His understated ebullience and warmth on the bandstand were not a spotlight sham. He felt a strong bond of friendship with everyone who danced to his music, whether he was playing in the sophisticated atmosphere of the Waldorf or in the heart of America at the Iowa Grange. He shook hands and spoke to each person who came up to say hello. These were his friends, and he treated them with the respect and admiration that he felt for them. He signed autographs and smiled because he was happy, and he gave a share of this happiness to everyone he met. Wherever he appeared he created his own world, and everyone in it shared the secret of his success.

His public image protected the mercurial man who lived beneath the studded, lace-tucked shirt and black tie. He was an unpredictable kaleidoscope of surprises. He was as beguiling as a child in his openness and honesty, and, without compromising his sophistication, he manifested a sparkling sense of humor and fast-paced wit. His mind was quick and intuitive, and the sound of his laughter was like baritone bubbles from vintage champagne.

The contrapuntal melodies of his character were inexorably entwined to make the music of his life, but the tune, be it playful or pompous, was always underscored by the fortissimo of his strength. The powerfully built, barrel-chested man was the recognized patriarch of a closely-knit Italian family. Rigidly disciplined himself, he expected it of others. He was a man of unquestioned authority who got what he wanted without demanding it, and in matters of importance did not offer choices. Having been exposed to the vagaries of success for many years, he was neither bitter nor suspicious, but rather cautious and wise. Whatever he did, he did with conviction.

To his devoted fans he was the greatest Italian since Caesar. As Caesar conquered Gaul, Lombardo conquered a nation with his music. Beneath a somewhat sterile public profile, the lion roared. Like Caesar, he made most of his decisions alone and took little counsel from his associates, a mixed blessing which at times affected his fortune. Forceful and arrogant, he ran his musical dynasty singlehandedly. He suffered financial setbacks, personal losses and disappointments like anyone else, but his attitude toward life was as stable as his music.

At the age of seventy-five, the bandleader was still a handsome and awesomely attractive man. He never lost his sparkle or his vitality. He greeted each day with excitement and anticipation. He extracted a full measure of joy from every hour and loved every minute he lived. Whether it was a good meal, a new song, an old friend or a sunset, he was completely caught up in it to the exclusion of everything else. He was totally attentive to the present. Everyone who met him was the most important person in his life at that moment.

That was his magic. He was totally involved in "now." It was this attitude that spared both him and his music from the ravages of time. He moved in a realm of agelessness. His bouncy gait when he was in front of the band conveyed this message to the millions of people who danced to his music. His personal optimism quite possibly touched and affected more lives in a lifetime than any other living American.

This is the legacy he left, and this is the legend his music will generate forever. Guy is telling everyone not to live *for* the moment, but to live *in* it. Let every day be New Year's Eve, and every night an opening.

It is the legacy he left me. My life was one of the many touched by him. It became richer, more rewarding, and so much more fruitful. I am proud to have been accepted by him as a close friend these many glorious years.

The Tradition

It has been said that should Guy Lombardo and the Royal Canadians fail to play "Auld Lang Syne" at midnight on New Year's Eve, a deep uneasiness would run through a large amount of the American people and a sudden hush would come over their Canadian neighbors, a conviction, despite evidence to the contrary on every calendar, that the New Year had not really arrived. Such was the nostalgia generated by Guy Lombardo.

It was not confined to New Year's Eve but was evident in every corner of America and Canada where Guy sent soothing messages to lovers and devoted fans with "the sweetest music this side of heaven." That devotion was most dramatically shown in February 1967, when Guy was operated on by Dr. Michael DeBakey at the Houston Methodist Hospital. Truckloads of flowers and telegrams deluged him during his convalescence. He had to change his room three times and take an assumed name in order to get his much needed rest. Ten days later the beloved bandleader continued his annual tour of the country to sold-out houses with standing-room only.

It is true that Guy Lombardo owned New Year's Eve in a very unique and individual way. It is true that Presidents Franklin Roosevelt, Harry Truman, Dwight D. Eisenhower, Lyndon B. Johnson, Richard Nixon, and Jimmy Carter have all called Guy on New Year's Eve to convey their best wishes on "Lombardo's Day." It is true that families, sweethearts, travelers, and lonely souls all over the world found a personal solace from the strains of Lombardo's "Auld Lang Syne" on New Year's Eve. It is true that thousands of Guy Lombardo New Year's Eve parties were held throughout the country at which time, to the tune of good food and wine and the sound of the Lombardo music, friends renewed their good neighbor affiliations, and looked forward to the new year with hope and optimism.

But it is not true that Guy Lombardo and the Royal Canadians existed only on New Year's Eve; Guy Lombardo's Royal Canadians are

13

truly a band for all seasons. The musicians have traveled in their chartered bus some 80,000 miles a year covering the United States coast to coast and countless towns in Canada. On the road nine months of the year, they spent the other three months at Jones Beach where the ever-active Guy produced musical spectaculars at the Jones Beach Theatre. And somehow Lombardo still found some spare time to record, endorse products, officiate at regatta and speedboat races, and make TV and radio appearances.

Many records of achievement in various fields have been set by Lombardo, and many of them are destined to remain unchallenged.

—As a recording star, he sold over 450 million records, more than any living artist in history.

—As a TV performer, he played to record-breaking numbers of viewers on television. It is estimated that each New Year's Eve drew an audience in excess of 55 million viewers. Since he began these TV parties in 1954, he amassed an outstanding total of over one and a quarter billion viewers, the longest continuing TV special in the industry's history to this day.

—He played at every Presidential inauguration since FDR's in 1933, setting another record.

—He introduced over 400 hit songs, more than any other band has ever done.

—As a sportsman, he personally broke all speedboat records during the 1946-52 period in his famous "Tempo."

—As a touring attraction, he traveled more miles (over 40 million) and played in more cities, towns, and hamlets than any other performer.

—Radio has also felt the effect of the Lombardo touch: 1927 found the Lombardo band the first radio sponsorship (Wrigley Chewing Gum) via WBBM in Chicago, and shortly thereafter the

first network radio pickup with the addition of Florsheim Shoes in Saint Paul.

—As a producer, Guy was more consistent than any other in American history. The summer of 1977 was the 24th consecutive year in which he successfully produced his million-dollar musical spectaculars at the 8200-seat Jones Beach Theatre in Wantagh, Long Island. No other producer in American history can match this achievement.

—As a businessman, he participated in more outside activities than any other performer. His diversified interests included oil, speedboat racing, a restaurant, an air charter service, a candy company, musical show production, TV production and syndication, land development, and boat manufacturing.

Guy was consistent not only in his achievements but in every aspect of his life. Brothers Carmen and Lebert, George Gowans, Freddie Kreitzer, Jim Dillon, and Muff Henry were with the band since its London, Ontario, inception. Saxophone player-turned-manager Larry Owen, joined the band in the late 1920's and remained as musical arranger until his retirement in 1977. Bus driver Don Byrnes, now functioning as road manager, had been aboard sixteen years. Guy had the same press agent for twenty-five years. Connie Andrus, secretary to the Royal Canadians for more than 40 years, still makes out the pay roll, arranges transportation, and acts as general den mother for the group. His consistency even extended to his talent representation, Music Corporation of America. Their association lasted thirty-five years until M.C.A. left the talent field to concentrate on production. Dave Baumgarten, formerly with M.C.A. represents the band through his Agency for the Performing Arts.

Guy celebrates his first New Year's Eve at New York's Waldorf-Astoria Hotel with actresses Lisa Loughlin, Nancy Dussault and Nai Bonet.

Dennis The Menace

Reprinted by permission of Field Enterprises, Inc.

"WE WAS WATCHIN' THIS NEW PROGRAM WITH **GUY LOMBARDO**... BUT SHE FELL ASLEEP."

Guy's first TV movie found him with Joan Collins in a scene from the Ellery Queen Series in 1973. The mystery show revolved around the murder of a night club patron celebrating New Year's Eve 1947.

In the early days, transportation for the band consisted of trains, buses, propeller planes, and cars that sometimes broke down.

CARNEGIE HALL/78th Season
Wednesday evening, December 3, 1969 at 8:30

Columbia Theatrical Enterprises, Inc.
a Subsidiary of
COLUMBIA ARTISTS MANAGEMENT INC.

Proudly Presents

GUY LOMBARDO
and his
ROYAL CANADIANS

Featuring

Carmen, Lebert & Victor Lombardo

The Twin Pianos

Lombardo Trio

Cliff Grass

Tony Cointreau

With Special Guest Artist

TONIA BERN CAMPBELL

Columbia Artists Management Inc.
Personal Direction: Charles K. Jones
165 West 57th Street, New York, N.Y. 10019

Capitol and Decca Records

C3

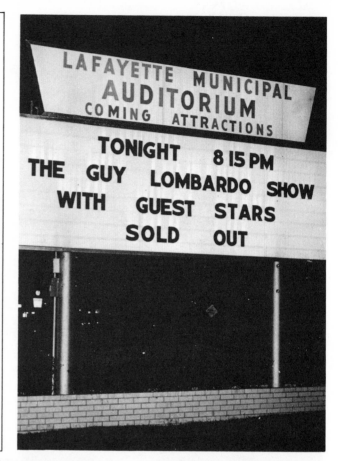

Carnegie Hall, Presidential Inaugurals, World's Fairs, and small towns throughout the U.S.A., they were all of the same importance to the Royal Canadians.

The road was not always as glamorous as it seemed. Sometimes stranded by unaccommodating vehicles, restaurants that were not always fancy, worried that he wouldn't be on time for the concert, Guy always found that the welcome awaiting them made it all worthwhile.

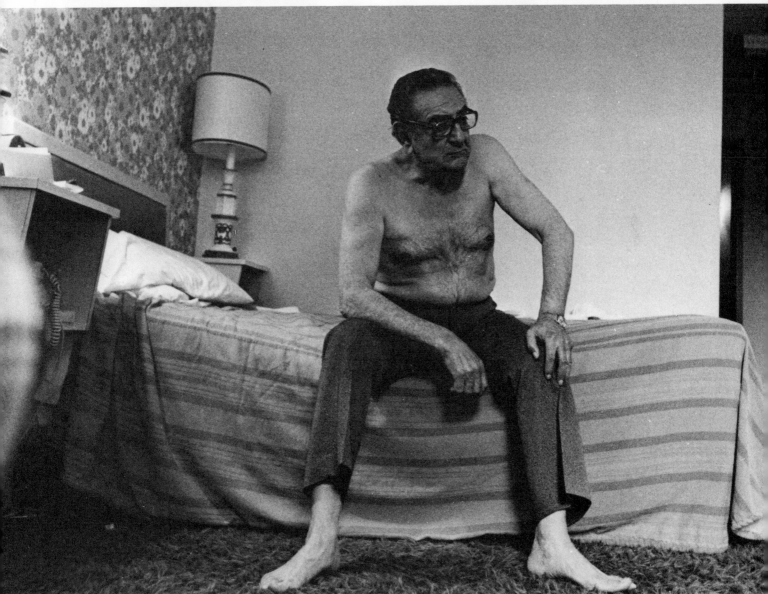

Autographs, handshakes and happy faces always awaited Guy during his annual cross-country tours.

24

Record crowds turned out at the Montreal Expo-67 when Gov. Rockefeller selected the Royal Canadians to represent him during the Fair's salute to New York State.

Guy was selected as King of The New Orleans Mardi Gras.

Kathy Nolan helps Guy in his capacity of Honorary Chairman of the Christmas Seal Campaign in 1970.

Guy Lombardo Day is declared at the New York World's Fair.

With pride, Guy accepts an honorary Doctorate of Music from Western Ontario University.

Guy picks out the winner of New York State Million Dollar Lottery.

The Navy presents Guy with an award for his interest on behalf of safety in boating.

The New York Drama Desk presents special award to Guy for twenty-four years of outstanding productions at Jones Beach and for his contributions to the American musical theatre.

Attending a Jerry Lewis Telethon represents one of the many activities of Guy on behalf of fund-raising drives and benefit shows.

Guy is made an honorary locomotive engineer for the Long Island Railroad.

Family

Guy was born in 1902 to Gaetano and Angelina Lombardo, who had immigrated from Italy to London, Ontario, where the elder Lombardo was a successful tailor. From the very beginning, music was a way of life for the Lombardo family. When Carmen and Lebert and Gaetano (later changed to Guy) were old enough (and later Victor, Joseph, Rose Marie, and Elaine) Papa and Momma very often joined them in vocal harmony after dinner. Their parents insisted that all the boys play a musical instrument and attend a musical school. The elder Lombardo was also the owner of the first motorboat in town, and this started Guy's interest in the most exciting aspect of his life, speedboat racing.

Papa Lombardo admonished his children, "Be the best. Always be the best." And he added, "Whatever you do in life, always give the people for whom you are working a little more and stay a few minutes longer than you are paid to stay." These words of advice were Guy's theme almost as much as "Auld Lang Syne."

One of the major turning points in Guy's life was the death of his brother Carmen. In addition to his soft tenor sax, which contributed so much to the identifiable sound of the Royal Canadians, Carmen was also a prolific tune-smith. He wrote many hit songs such as "Seems Like Old Times," "Boo-Hoo," "Return to Me," "Sweethearts On Parade," "Little Coquette," "A Sailboat In The Moonlight," "Powder Your Face With Sunshine," and "Snuggle On Your Shoulder." He was more than just a brother to Guy. They were inseparable at home and in their travels; close socially, psychologically, and professionally. During the agonizing period when Carmen was ill with cancer, with tears in his eyes, Guy said to his wife Lilliebell, "If Carm dies, how can I go on? I shall give up the band." As though anticipating his brother's feelings, Carmen whispered a message to his devoted wife Florence before he died: "Tell Guy the band will be bigger and more popular than ever. Tell him to do it for me." And when Carmen died in 1971, although it was the saddest day in Guy's life, it also gave him the determination to continue the legend of the Royal Canadians, reaching greater heights of popularity than ever before; and the many hits from Carmen's prolific pen remain among the most requested tunes from the vast repertoire of the Royal Canadians. There is never a night on tour when a request for one of Carmen's familiar numbers is not made by members of the audience.

The house in London, Ontario, Canada, where Guy was born in 1902.

Momma Lombardo

Poppa Lombardo

Carmen, Guy, Lebert, and their mother at their childhood home in London, Ontario, Canada.

Carmen, Guy, Lebert.

Guy and his violin.

Guy, age 12; Carmen, 10, in their debut in 1914.

The Lombardos picnic outside their London, Ontario home.

Guy at 7 just before he started music lessons.

Carmen at 13 and sister Elaine, 10.

Opposite page: The Lombardo brothers stroll the boardwalk after a performance, Atlantic City, 1931.

Opposite page: The brothers on Guy's first yacht, Tempo, 1934.

Below: Publicity photos were part of the game on the sand dunes of Long Island.

Left: Rose Marie, Carmen and Guy concentrate on their radio script.

1901   1951

Mr. and Mrs. Guy Lombardo, Jr.

Mr. and Mrs. Carmen Lombardo

Mr. Lebert Lombardo

Mr. and Mrs. Kenneth Gardner

Mr. and Mrs. Victor Lombardo

Mr. Joseph Lombardo

Miss Rose Marie Lombardo

request the pleasure of your company

at the celebration of the

Fiftieth Wedding Anniversary

of their parents

Mr. and Mrs. Guy Lombardo

Sunday, the nineteenth of August

from four o'clock

Stonehenge

Hillcrest Park, Stamford, Connecticut

R.S.V.P.

The Lombardos announce the Golden Anniversary of their parents, Angelina and Guy, Sr., and celebrate the occasion.

Above: *Roosevelt Grill, 1954, finds the Lombardo clan gathering to celebrate the band's continuing success.*

Below: *The Lombardos gather to celebrate the wedding of Rose Marie, who sang with the band for two years.*

The Making of
The Lombardo Band

It may have begun in London, Ontario, when Guy, still in grammar school, organized a four-piece band that played at church socials. It was expanded when its young leader reached his teens. The group achieved moderate success and soon, to their frightened surprise, an American booking agent got them a job in Cleveland.

Perhaps the most formative experience of the Lombardo career occurred in 1923, when the Lombardos made their first U.S. appearance at the Claremont Cafe, in Cleveland, Ohio. The advice of Louis Bleet, the owner, helped mold the band, and at least one of his suggestions made musical history. It stemmed from a complaint.

"People complain that they ask you to play a number and you don't get around to it for a long time, maybe not at all," Bleet told Guy one night. "What's the matter?"

"Sometimes we have so many requests that we just can't play them all," Guy explained.

"Hmm," Bleet said. "Yeah, I see. If you played every request it would take you all night, wouldn't it? But why do you have to play a complete three-minute orchestration of every number everybody requests? One chorus would be enough. That way everybody could get what they wanted and get it right away, too."

"But you can't play one chorus of a song, stop, play another chorus, stop, and go on like that all night," Guy protested. "It would be too jerky."

"I don't mean for you to stop," Bleet said. "Keep right on playing, but play a different song."

"We couldn't do that!" exclaimed the twenty-two year old leader. "One song might be in a different key from the one before it. Or it might be in a different tempo."

"You could have Freddie Kreitzer play a few chords on the piano to modulate from one key to another," Bleet suggested. "While he's at it, he could change the tempo, too."

Guy shook his head. "I don't think anybody ever did anything like that before," he said. But then, as Bleet started nervously biting his thumb, Guy quickly added, "But I'll talk to Freddie about it and see what we can do."

Above: *The Lombardo band played the Stork Club in London, Ontario, on New Year's Eve, 1921. The personnel of the band, with a few additions, would remain basically unchanged.*
Below: *Their first record session in Indianapolis, 1924.*

Above: *An early photograph of the Royal Canadians–the faces that would continue to appear through the band's decades of popularity.*
Below: *Hotel Roosevelt, 1930, with Fred Hickman and Larry Owen.*

Above: *The Royal Canadians on the set of Paramount Pictures for the filming of "Many Happy Returns" in 1934.*

54

Still in Hollywood and Guy's violin was not just a prop.

The band was the number one record seller and the recording sessions were more and more frequent.

Most of the young orchestras getting started in the 1920's followed a fairly set procedure. They bought stock arrangements, rehearsed them a couple of times and that was it, nothing added, nothing taken away. The Lombardo group, from the beginning, was unique in that it devised its own arrangements. You might think that Guy's sound taste and desire for perfection or Carmen's great musical knowledge and interest were behind this. Actually it was all because of the new man on trumpet, Lebert Lombardo.

"I couldn't hit the high notes on those stock arrangements," Lebert confesses today, still showing traces of chagrin after fifty years. "I'd only been playing the trumpet a short while, I'd never had any formal lessons, and I didn't have a big range. I don't have an extremely wide range today, as a matter of fact, but then it was nothing at all. So what we would do, instead of buying the orchestral arrangements, was to get the vocal

arrangements. These were usually set in a lower key, and I could find my way a little more easily."

But this type of arrangement had to be embellished for a full orchestra, and thus began an institution, the famous Lombardo rehearsals. The band by that time numbered nine men, with Guy playing the violin and conducting. There were two saxophones, one trumpet, one trombone, piano, drums, guitar and bass. The membership was almost set. Of the nine men who would remain with the band for over thirty years, seven were on hand, the three Lombardos, Freddie Kreitzer, George Gowans, Jim Dillon and Muff Henry. All of them were eager, enthusiastic, and searching. Working up a number was both a labor of love and lot of fun.

One of the reasons for the great popularity of the Lombardo band over the years is the fact that it is distinguishable from all other bands. Turning your radio dial or flicking your TV tuner, you can

Left: The Steel Pier in Atlantic City, 1932.
Right: *The Strand Theatre in N.Y.C., where Guy Lombardo and the Royal Canadians enjoyed record-shattering engagements.*

always tell in the first second or two if it's Lombardo. This is a phenomenon the Lombardo band shares with only a few other institutions and individuals. You can recognize a Bing Crosby or an Arthur Godfrey or a Cary Grant the moment he opens his mouth. These stars have an indefinable something that sets them apart. Few groups can combine to achieve the magical quality of a distinct sound, but this is exactly what the Lombardos have done. Further, they have maintained it for fifty years. And it all began back in Cleveland, Ohio, in 1923.

A second factor of the Lombardo Sound, an ingredient of equal importance, involves the individual tones which make up the whole. The way Guy explained this is to begin with just the opposite of the Lombardo sound, with what musicians call the "legitimate tone". If you go to several musical shows on Broadway, or listen to sound tracks of musical films, you will note that

the orchestras all sound alike. And well they should, for they are all composed of the fine musicians who have developed their art to the fullest extent. These artists are so good that they are interchangeable. Any one instrumentalist in any one orchestra would be able to play in any other.

But when the two men who set the standard for the Lombardo sound (Carmen for the reed instruments and Lebert for the brass) did the "legitimate tone," they sounded different somehow. If it was necessary to describe the tone of either one as better or worse than the "legitimate tone" then the word would have to be "worse," although, as Carmen once wryly pointed out, if he had had a "legitimate tone" he might have been playing in an orchestra pit for $150 a week instead of with the Lombardo band for many times that. Actually, Carmen had the greatest admiration for modern musicians. When he was

Hundreds of thousands of the photos were purchased by Guy Lombardo
fans at five cents each from photo-dispensing machines.

Ever sartorially in style, the Fashion Foundation of America and other fashion experts frequently included Guy on their Best Dressed list.

Right page: *Lebert and Carmen going over some music before the evening's performance of the band.*

getting started there were only a few truly superb musicians. Today there are thousands. He explained, "I'm afraid if I had to compete with them for jobs in other orchestras, I'd starve."

The classical tone in the reed instrument is described by musicians as being "compact." By contrast the tenor sax tone is full and rich. Carmen used a lot of vibrato; he was an emotional player; he gave his instrument all he had, including body English. He played from his toes up; and he honestly meant every note. His playing was unabashedly sentimental. Though it was different, Carmen's style was not too difficult for another good saxophone or clarinet player to follow. It took a little time for the band to get used to Carmen's replacement after his death, but the Royal Canadians still retain the same sound today.

What the Lombardo band did to slow songs down was simply a matter of arithmetic. They made every note twice as long. This by no means made the song slow or draggy, but rather en-

hanced its rhythm and its message. Of course, they also played some fast numbers and they frequently used the less familiar schottische rhythm, which has become a Lombardo trademark over the years.

And so the Lombardo brothers' orchestra developed their sound, a repertory of numbers, and the quality of musicianship that comes with talent and application. It could have gone in other directions had they not listened to Mr. Bleet that eventful day in 1923 when the wide-eyed youngsters fresh out of their London, Ontario, shell opened at the Claremont Cafe in Cleveland, Ohio.

Then came the big decision. Though a bit worried and filled with youthful concern, the band voted to remain in the States. Having already achieved a distinctive style, so much that his music was easily identifiable to listeners, Guy went about exploiting his music on radio, which was then in its infancy. Guy persuaded the owner of a Cleveland radio station to give him time on

the air every night at his own expense. The band's rhythms were thus aired to the outskirts of Cleveland. They began gaining attention, which finally resulted in a booking into Cleveland's Music Box. It was while performing at the Music Box that Guy met and fell in love with Lilliebell Glenn, who shortly thereafter became his wife. This began a partnership that endured throughout his lifetime, and Lilliebell Lombardo remains the Royal Canadians' biggest booster.

The real break for the band came in Chicago in 1927 when they were booked into a club called The Granada Cafe on the south side of town, opposite a cemetery. The opening was a disaster. Finally after six forgettable weeks of slow business, Lombardo persuaded the Club's owner to run a wire into the ballroom so the band could be broadcast fifteen minutes each evening over the radio station WBBM. Radio had worked for Guy in Cleveland. He decided to see if this new gadget might now give them the boost they needed in Chicago. The first show went over the

air on a cold Wednesday evening in November. Before they finished the fifteen-minute spot, the station called and asked them to play all night. By midnight the club was filled to overflowing. The next morning they had two radio sponsors and the band that was unknown on Wednesday afternoon, was the talk of Chicago by Thursday morning.

A year and a half later in 1929, Jules Stein, who founded the best-known band agency in the country, Music Corporation of America, brought Guy Lombardo and the Royal Canadians into New york. They opened at the Roosevelt Grill on October 3, 1929, two days before the stock market crashed. The engagement lasted thirty-three years.

As time went on, there came huge commercial radio programs, the first being "The Robert Burns Cigar Show." Guy introduced Burns and Allen for the first time on this program. Later came the prestigious Standard oil of New Jersey account, which combined a tour with radio

Lilliebell Lombardo was always there to boost the band, join in the campaign during World War II to "Save Fats For Victory" and to accompany Guy on his many tours throughout the country. The beauty from Cleveland gave Guy the support he needed at a time when the Lombardos were almost ready to turn back to their London, Ontario beginnings.

Guy, Lilliebell and Rowdy on board Tempo, 1955.

Radio broadcasts and greeting old friends from the podium each night attested to the continuing success of the band.

broadcasts emanating from various cities. The shows from the Grill were broadcast on radio over WABC, but by the end of the year the other two networks wanted to do a New Year's Eve show from the hotel. As a result, Guy rang out the old year for CBS and rang in the new one for NBC. He was on the air every New Year's Eve after that.

In 1931 the Royal Canadians broke every ballroom record and in 1933 they conquered Hollywood. That year they appeared at the Los Angeles Coconut Grove. Their fame and success were assured. Celebrities and movie stars flocked to dance to the most imitated band of the day. Every evening seemed like a film set come to life. It was normal for Lombardo to spy such luminaries as Clark Gable, Norma Shearer, Irving Thalberg, Joan Crawford, Jeanette MacDonald, Franchot Tone, Errol Flynn, Ronald Coleman, Jean Harlow, Ginger Rogers, Nelson Eddy, virtually the "Who's Who" of filmdom, dancing to the tunes of the Royal Canadians. The following year the band made its first film, *Many Happy Returns,* in which they were reunited with George Burns and Gracie Allen, who also starred in the movie.

One reason for Lombardo's success was his ability to spot forthcoming trends. It was Guy who first noticed the value of radio syndication, resulting in the orchestra's making "The Guy Lombardo Show" one of the most successful of all radio programs. It was the maestro, too, who first developed a perfect formula for the presentation of a dance orchestra on TV. Where other musical groups had failed, Lombardo went to NBC-TV's New York station in November 1953 with a program presenting his orchestra playing dance music for diners and dancers, and generally doing what they normally do in a dining room or dance hall. The result was a tremendously successful and critically acclaimed series.

By 1941 all the Lombardo clan were living on Long Island, and their parents had moved from Canada to Stamford, Connecticut. Carmen was writing hit songs. Lebert, who had begun as a drummer before he taught himself to play the trumpet, had developed into one of the leading trumpet players in the business. Young Victor sat in the sax section of the band. Kenny Gardner, who would soon marry Lombardo's sister, Elaine, joined the band as a vocalist in 1942.

It was truly a family affair. Sixteen-year-old Rose Marie Lombardo also took her place on the bandstand as a singer, but left the band after two years to marry and raise a family. Victor, who left the group to form his own band, had now retired

Above: Guy and Ed Sullivan while the latter was interviewing the maestro in Atlantic City in 1935 for the New York Daily News.
Below: Film stars greet Guy and welcome him to Hollywood.

Above: *Guy joins Joan Crawford and Franchot Tone for a glass of champagne at the Coconut Grove in Hollywood, 1933.*
Below: *Jean Harlow and Guy share a table at the Coconut Grove.*

Celebrities were also Guy's friends, and there was always a handful whenever Guy played New York or California.

Fred Allen and his wife Portland

Alan Ladd

Laraine Day

Gregory Peck

Dorothy Lamour

Ralph Edwards

Dorothy Kirsten

Bob Hope

Dinah Shore

Eddie Cantor

Phil Baker

Shelley Winters

Eddie "Duffy's Tavern" Gardner

Perry Como

Martin Block

Buddy Clarke and daughter, Penny.

George Burns and Gracie Allen were introduced to radio by Guy.

Below: "Many Happy Returns," Guy's first film, also featured George Burns and Gracie Allen and Ray Milland (behind Burns) in his first leading role.

Right: Guy (shown with Mindy Carson) was extremely active in radio, touring for Esso and Lucky Strike throughout the country.

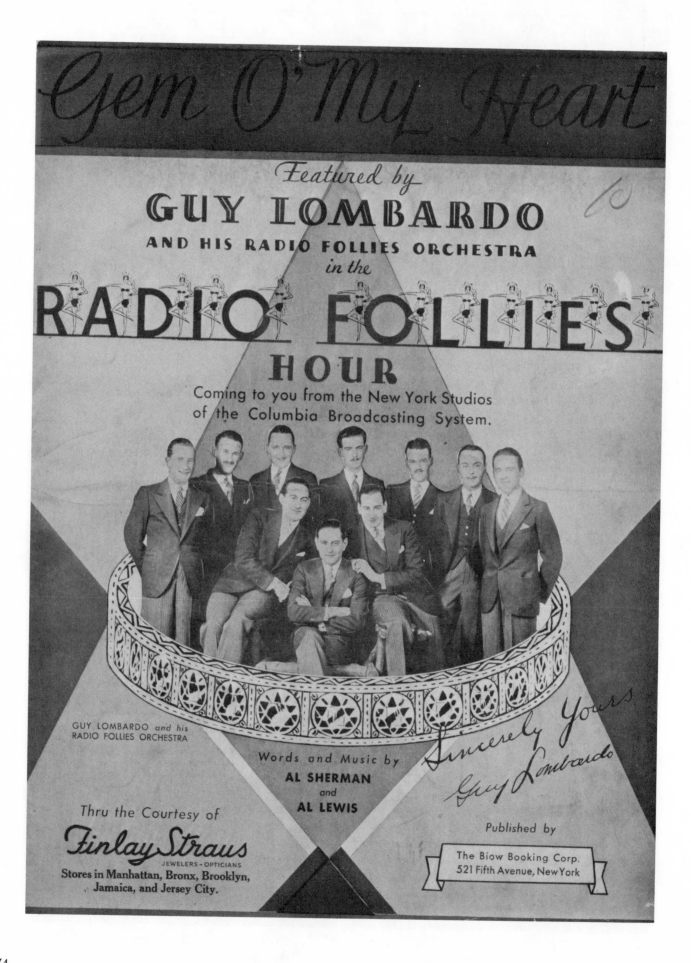

THE SWEETEST MUSIC THIS SIDE OF HEAVEN
Lyrics by CLIFF FRIEND • Music by CARMEN LOMBARDO
GUY LOMBARDO & HIS ROYAL CANADIANS • BURNS & ALLEN
in PARAMOUNT'S "MANY HAPPY RETURNS"
FARE THEE WELL
THE SWEETEST MUSIC THIS SIDE OF HEAVEN
THE BOOGIE MAN
Famous Music Corporation
1619 BROADWAY NEW YORK
PUBLISHERS TO PARAMOUNT PICTURES
Made in U.S.A.

A television show being taped live at the Lombardo's East Point House restaurant on Long Island, 1955.

to Florida. Kenny Gardner has also retired and lives in Plainview, Long Island, where he is the head of the Volunteer Fire Department. The only non-musical member of the family, Joseph Lombardo, was considered by Guy to be the most successful. He has become a world-renowned antique dealer and spends much of his time traveling.

Nineteen fifty-four was another conspicuous year in the life of Guy Lombardo and the Royal Canadians. It was the beginning of network pickup of their New Year's Eve party at the Roosevelt Hotel. Later the party switched to the Grand Ballroom of the Waldorf Astoria via CBS-TV network and CBC-TV in Canada. These year-end parties continue on TV today.

With their success at the Roosevelt Grill assured, Guy and Lilliebell began apartment hunting in Manhattan. They heard that George Gershwin's Riverside Drive penthouse was becoming available as the brilliant composer was on his way to Hollywood to work on some film musicals. They grabbed it quickly. Not only was Gershwin one of Lombardo's friends, but he was the composer of one of Guy's favorite scores, "Porgy and Bess."

Lilliebell became a great party thrower during their stay in Manhattan. The penthouse was always filled with songwriters, musicians, and inevitably one or two hard-working song pluggers. They were happy nights and the Lombardos somehow knew that George Gershwin would approve of those melodious get-togethers at his domicile. The news of his untimely death in Hollywood at the age of thirty-three saddened all of them. The parties somehow never quite retained the spirit they had before his passing.

It was shortly thereafter that they purchased a piece of land in Freeport, Long Island at the foot of South Grove Street. It was at that spot they docked "Tempo" and made the boat their summer home. Then with the aid of brother Joe, a brilliant architect, plans were formulated for a permanent home on the land adjacent to their "on-the-water" residence. They lived there thirty-five years. In due time the famous Guy Lombardo East Point House restaurant was added to the estate. For years Guy and Lilliebell supervised this famous sea food emporium on the water. The countless twin lobsters, Lobsters Lombardo, and other menu favorites that were served to thousands of East Point House regulars

Kenny Gardner, who began the vocals in 1942, was first brought to the attention of Guy when Elaine heard him on radio. Kenny and Elaine married during the war.

The Lombardo brothers welcome their new vocalist, Rose Marie Lombardo in 1943, the only regular female vocalist the band ever had.

are but a memory now, since the restaurant was burned to the ground by a tragic fire in 1960.

The Lombardo house in Freeport was a happy home. It was here, to the houseful of Lilliebell's beloved dogs and cats, that Guy came for his jaunts in the luxurious "Tempo" and to spearhead his summer productions at Jones Beach. It was the solid support of Lilliebell and the permanence of the Freeport home that gave Guy the enthusiasm and the "looking ahead" attitude which accounts for the continuing success of the Royal Canadians.

It's interesting to note the advertising copy used by the Roosevelt Hotel in its first newspaper ad announcing the acquisition of Guy Lombardo and the Royal Canadians. Lombardo's friend Ralph Hitz from Cleveland was now managing the brand new New Yorker Hotel, and he wanted them. So did the St. Regis. So did the Roosevelt. The Lombardos spent weeks studying the geographical and social patterns of New York, as well as the floor plans of the hotels in question. They felt that their most ardent fans were the young college crowd, and they finally decided to choose the room where the college kids would be the most welcome. This eliminated the New Yorker, which, located on the edge of the garment district, attracted a commercial clientele. On the other hand, they felt that the St. Regis, with its social-register crowd, would be a little too sophisticated. The Roosevelt was in between the two. Furthermore they liked the layout of the Roosevelt Grill, the room in which they would play. And so the choice was made. The repercussions were felt long afterward. Hitz, the New Yorker's manager, was so resentful that for years he refused to hire artists represented by Guy's agents, M.C.A.

Thus, on October 3, 1929, the initial Roosevelt newspaper ad described the band as follows:

"The sweetest music this side of heaven . . . it has been said of the dance music of GUY LOMBARDO that it smoulders and glows like a living coal . . . now soft with a lilting cadence of a dreamy melody . . . now vivid with pulsating jazz rhythms. In turn seductive and tumultuous, alternately tender and unrestrained, it is proving the season's outstanding musical sensation."

Such ad copy for a band today would probably result in both the band and the members of

Above Left: *Rose Marie's first publicity photo, appropriate for Valentine's Day.*

Above Right: *Rose Marie, Guy, and Kenny Gardner are cited for their efforts on behalf of Army recruiting.*

Right: *Rose Marie rehearses a vocal number with her brothers.*

Opposite page: *Rose Marie with the band in the early forties at the Roosevelt Grill in New York City.*

Masquerade Party to celebrate their new home in Freeport, Long Island.

the Madison Avenue agency being run out of town, but it certainly was not the case at that time. Thus began a relationship that lasted for thirty-three years until the winter of 1963. That third of a century at the Roosevelt spanned several different eras, the roaring twenties, the Depression years, the war and the post-war days of the forties, fifties and early sixties. The relationship between the orchestra and management was always warm.

It is interesting to note that many years after the first announcement appeared in the papers heralding the advent of the Royal Canadians at the Roosevelt Hotel, a somewhat more realistic approach was written for *Variety* by the *New York Daily News'* Ben Gross, retired dean of New York radio and television editors. Ben wrote:

"The night of Thursday, October 3, 1929, was a historical one, but I didn't know it.

"That was the evening Guy Lombardo and his Royal Canadians opened in the Grill of the Hotel Roosevelt. At first, it seemed much like any other opening of those hectic days. After all, there were some pretty good bands around at the time; Whiteman, Lopez, to name just two; and so those of us who were present at Madison and 45th had no reason to suspect that this occasion would be a memorable one...

"Anyway, I was there. And probably no other radio editor of today can make that claim.

"I shall always recall the effect Guy's first number had on the audience. It was rhythmic, it was gay, but it had a soothing quality. The customers not only danced, but also listened. There was talk about the band playing "off pitch," an assertion that Lombardo firmly denies. But most of those present had one comment, "This outfit's music is distinctive — it's unlike any others."

"And that's why I regard Lombardo as one of the smartest men in show business. Since his beginning, he has recognized that a trademark is a precious asset. Packers of ham, makers of toothpaste, know this. So do writers and composers. But in the dance band field, it is astounding how many leaders ignore this basic principle.

"I have heard thousands of bands since beginning to listen to radio professionally in 1925, but Lombardo has been one of the very few I could ever identify without the help of the announcer...

"Back in 1929, crowds used to gather around a bandstand merely to watch the orchestra or certain soloists perform. But it didn't happen that night at the Roosevelt. And it still doesn't because Guy always has had the notion that the people on the floor are out there because they

Guy and Lilliebell at Masquerade Party.

Guy and Lilliebell on the popular TV show "Masquerade Party."

Guy's and Lilliebel's 20th Wedding Anniversary celebrated at Chasen's in Los Angeles. Standing, the Lombardo brothers and Rose Marie, Fay Emerson and husband Elliot Roosevelt; second and third from left, Alan Ladd and his wife Sue Carroll; second from right, sitting, Mrs. Jules Stein.

Above: The sleek Tempo commuter, Guy's early express cruiser, parked outside his Freeport, Long Island home.
Below: Guy and Lilliebell enjoy their Freeport, Long Island home, which brother Joseph Lombardo designed.

Left: *Guy with Lilliebell's award-winning poodle, Suzy.*
Right: *Missie, who captured the hearts of Guy and Lilliebell after Suzy died.*

Above: Guy leads a group from his East Point House restaurant to Jones Beach where he presented outdoor musical extravaganzas for twenty-four years.
Below: Lilliebell "dancing it up" at the East Point House restaurant, which was run by Guy until it burned to the ground in 1966.

Above left: Guy and Satchmo "mix it up" at Jones Beach where they performed in Guy's production of "Mardi Gras." *Above right:* Guy and lobsterman-politician Perry Duryea check out the quality of the lobsters at the Jones Beach Theatre, 1967. *Below left:* Guy, Robert Moses and actor Paul Hartman enjoy the corn during Guy's production of "Showboat" in 1956. *Below right:* One of the reasons Guy's East Point House restaurant was such a success was that he knew and loved food.

Ethel Merman and 90-year old Eubie Blake congratulate Bill Lombardo ('Guy's nephew and Lebert's son) as he leads the band at the start of the second fifty years of the Royal Canadians.

want to dance. So he sees no reason for spotlighting an instrumentalist or vocalist for the sake of pleasing those who merely want to stare.

"Twenty years is a long time. I confess I wasn't thinking in long-range terms that evening at the Roosevelt in 1929. I merely knew that the music was good, and that I enjoyed it just as I shall when I attend Lombardo's 1969 opening.

"And come to think of it, that is about the highest tribute one may put to a dance band—to enjoy the music."

Guy Lombardo and his Royal Canadians became the most listened to, talked about, and imitated big band of all time. Why? For a time even its leader didn't know. "We didn't realize what we had," Guy once said during a discussion of his band's early days. "We had to ask people what it was they liked about the band."

They didn't have to ask for long. It soon became evident what it was that people liked about "the sweetest music this side of heaven"—it had superb tempos and produced a succession of steady, unobtrusive beats that make it a pleasure to go out on the floor and move around. Anyone who could dance at all, could dance to the Lombardo music.

Lombardo's band was also a great band to

talk to. It never played so loudly that one dancer had to say "What?" when another dancer spoke to him. And Lombardo plays wonderful tunes, for, with his years of experience, he knew how to select numbers that created a cozy, intimate mood. Lombardo believed implicitly in his music and succeeded handsomely in selling it to generations of dancers and listeners.

More than any other band, Guy Lombardo's Royal Canadians based its success, purely and simply, on a securely set style. "The big trick," admitted Guy, "is to be recognized without an announcer telling you who it is!"

Even though they started developing the formula in the early 1920s in their hometown, they never changed as they made successive and successful steps forward.

Nineteen sixty-nine has come and gone. Nineteen-eighty approaches and people are still dancing to the music of Guy Lombardo's Royal Canadians. They come, not to shake, rattle and roll or to ventilate their anxiety or pent-up hostilities, but to hold each other in their arms and dance. It happened October 3, 1929, and it has been happening ever since, and it is happening now, under the direction of Guy's nephew, Lebert's thirty-year-old son, Bill Lombardo.

cal treat of the night, at which time Guy and his Royal Canadians put on a musical duet with Louis Armstrong and his quartet. "Satchmo" loved it so much he came back the second year and helped inaugurate the Schaefer dance tent into which patrons could come after the show to dance and listen, free of charge, to both bands. The tradition continues today.

There followed seven years of the magic of Richard Rodgers and Oscar Hammerstein II. First came two summers of *South Pacific*, when the Jones Beach Theatre became the Island of Bali Hi, and the dramatic LST sailed on Zach's Bay as the warmhearted romance of Emile De Beque and Nellie Forbush unfolded.

This was followed by the two seasons of the all-time favorite, Richard Rodgers and Oscar Hammerstein's *The Sound of Music*. Guy transformed the theatre into Austria, complete with its mountains, the Von Trapp castle, and the replica of Nunnberg Abbey.

The King and I the following year changed the massive backstage sets from the alps of Austria to the spires of Siam, and its lagoon filled with royal barges, surrounded by the harem rooms, the schoolhouse, and the glittering ballroom.

Music of the calliope announced the coming of *Carousel* with a real-live midway and the largest working carousel ever seen on an American stage, along with a preview of heaven as seen through the imagination of set designer, John William Keck.

Oklahoma! was the final Rodgers and Hammerstein musical produced by Guy in this series; the corn grew as high as an elephant's eye right there on the stage of the Jones Beach theatre.

And so it continued each year to the production for the summer of 1977, the twenty-fourth (and last) for the bandleader-producer Guy Lombardo, when the leprechauns and elves came into the green forest to lend their magic to the Yip Harburg, Burton Lane, and Fred Saidy musical, *Finian's Rainbow*.

So many stars in these productions and so many who emerged from them as stars: the late Metropolitan Opera star, Lauritz Melchior, Joel Gray, Dom DeLuise, Arthur Treacher, William Gaxton, Constance Towers, John Cullum, Robert Clary, Jane Keene, Jerome Hines, Nancy Dussault, Andy Devine, Elaine Malbin, Kathy Nolan, Patricia Arnell, Nancy Andrews, Hal LeRoy, Jules Munshin, Fritz Weaver, Louis Armstrong, Elliot Gould, and many, many, more talented actors and actresses, dancers and singers who helped make these summer productions memorable.

When Robert Moses sold the idea of producing shows at Jones Beach to Guy, he may have given him an exciting way of life those many summers, a way of life that meant more to him than any other of his many accomplishments.

Below, left to right: Guy and Michael Todd, Jr. discuss "Around the World in 80 Days"; Guy with Joseph Stein, who wrote the book for "Fiddler On The Roof"; Guy with Robert Moses and Oscar Hammerstein II, who wrote the lyrics for Richard Rodgers' music; Yip Harburg points out one of the highlights of his "Finian's Rainbow"; Guy and Richard Rodgers talk over plans for the latter's musical, "The King And I." All of these musicals were among the many produced by Lombardo at the 8200-seat Jones Beach Theatre.

Magic scenery, colorful costumes and exciting ensemble dancing epitomized the Lombardo productions at Jones Beach for twenty-four glorious summers. Each night the show ended with a spectacular display of fireworks, followed by dancing to "the sweetest music this side of heaven" in the Schaefer dance tent.

Above: Animals were a special feature in some of the Lombardo productions, such as the elephant, a star of "Arabian Nights," seen here carrying Mary Martin while Lauritz Melchior acts as guide to Guy and Robert Moses.

Center left, top to bottom: An aerial view of the 8200-seat Jones Beach Theatre.

Robert Moses, Lebert, Carmen, Guy, Oscar Hammerstein II, and director John Kennedy gaze at the miniature set for Mr. Hammerstein's "Showboat," which Guy produced in 1956-7 and then again in 1976.

Massive construction begins for one of Guy's productions at Jones Beach Theatre, whose rear stage is larger than five regular Broadway prosceniums, and whose front stage is equal to three great White Way stages.

Center right, top to bottom: Land, sea and air are utilized to construct sets for Guy Lombardo productions

Rehearsals continue while sets are still under construction.

Film star, Elliot Gould, encircled, was a chorus boy in "Hit The Deck."

Realistic volcanoes erupt in "Paradise Island" and a real *full moon* rises over the theatre during a performance of Guy's "Arabian Nights."

Pirate ships, showboats, Norwegian floating palaces, boats from Arabian Nights fantasies, a highly publicized singing whale, were some of the marine-dominated props created by boat enthusiast Guy Lombardo for his productions.

Boats, water ballet, and ice skating beauties were part of the awe-inspiring sights and sounds at a Guy Lombardo production.

Montage of the world of Guy Lombardo as seen through the eyes of Jones Beach Theatre patrons.

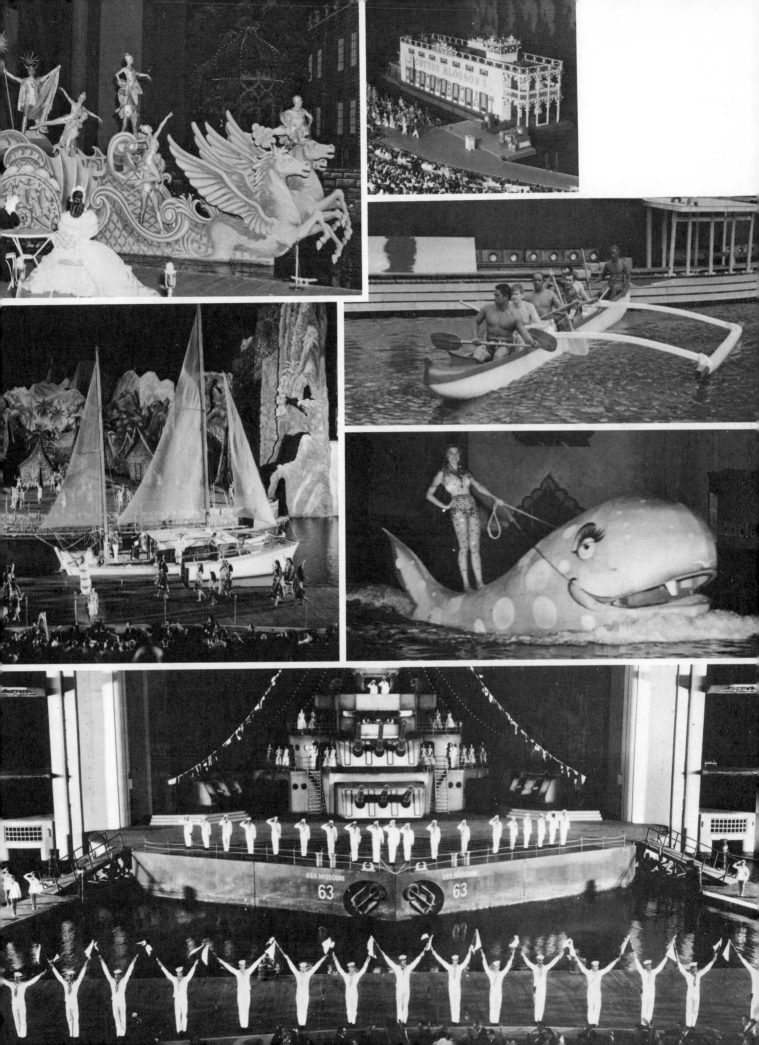

A capacity audience of 8,200 watch balloon float 150 feet in the air carrying stars Fritz Weaver, Robert Clary and Elaine Malbin during "Around The World In 80 Days."

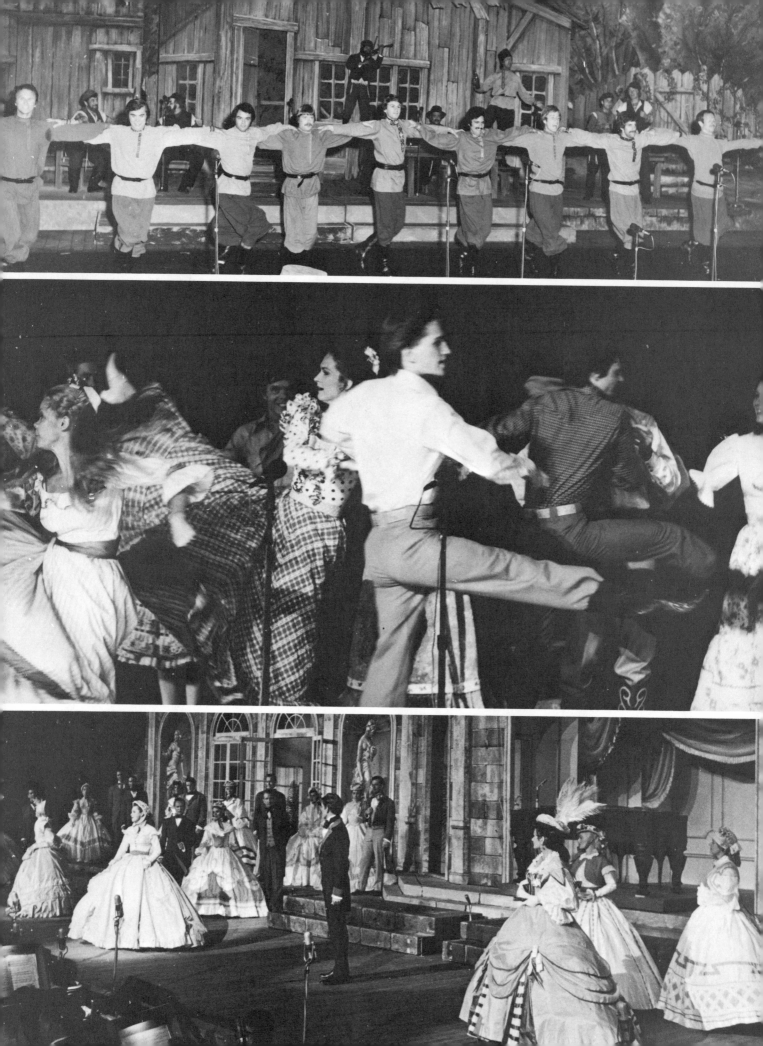

Guy mixes fun with business at Jones Beach. He participated in all aspects of these productions and enjoyed every minute of it. Authenticity was important to Guy, as when he flew 60 children from Hawaii for the production of "Paradise Island." He even went so far as to mix a little water from the South Pacific into Zach's Bay for his production of "South Pacific."

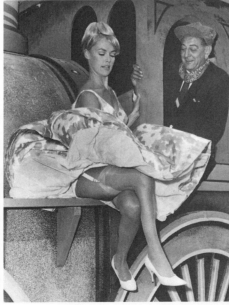

Scenes from Guy Lombardo Jones Beach musicals.

More scenes from Guy Lombardo Jones Beach musical

Artists who appeared in Guy's Jones Beach musicals and went on to stardom.

John Cullum

Elliot Gould

Nancy Dussault

Christine Andreas

Elliot Gould *was a chorus boy.*
Arthur Treacher *became a regular with Merv Griffin.*
Christine Andreas *went on as star of "My Fair Lady" revival on Broadway.*
Fritz Weaver *was selected to star in the Broadway show, "Baker Street."*
Bonnie Franklin *got her own TV series.*
Reid Shelton *became Daddy Warbucks in the hit musical, "Annie."*
Robert Clary *became one of "Hogan's Heroes."*
Joel Grey *was star of Broadway musical, "George M" and the film "Cabaret."*
Dom De Luise *went on to Hollywood and TV.*
John Cullum *left Jones Beach to star in the musical "Twentieth Century."*
Gail Benedict *is now featured in "Dancin'!"*
Constance Towers *starred opposite Yul Brynner on Broadway in "The King And I" after a similar role at Jones Beach.*
Jane Keane *from Jones Beach to "The Honeymooners" with Jackie Gleason.*
Barney Martin *to Broadway musicals and TV.*
Patricia Arnell *went on to become the star of the National Company of "Gigi."*
Nancy Dussault *went from Jones Beach "South Pacific" into TV commercials and "Side By Side By Sondheim" on Broadway.*

Dom De Luise

Jane Keane

Arthur Treacher

Robert Clary

Constance Towers

Fritz Weaver

Patricia Arnell

Joel Grey

Bonnie Franklin

Reid Shelton

Gail Benedict

Barney Martin

A Champion On The Water

Guy's crew prepares Tempo VII for the Detroit Memorial, 1955.

Little did Guy realize as a growing youngster of ten that his Dad's purchase of a motorboat would set the neighbors buzzing and his own mind churning. When young Gaetano saw his father zooming along the Thames in Ontario at the sensational speed of six miles an hour, it was the speed that impressed him, even though to Papa the boat was mainly a means to entertain his friends. The precious moment came for Guy when he was allowed to take over the wheel to spell the older men during a refreshment break. But even then he knew that boats and speedboat racing were destined to play an important role in his life. Guy reflected fondly on the trips in Papa's motor launch, as he counted his many trophies and looked at the record book extolling his speedboat racing achievements.

With his enthusiasm for boating growing as fast as his popularity, Lombardo began racing in 1942. When he won his first race, a marathon from Atlantic City to Cape May, he was hooked. Then came his second race in Cincinnati. Once again, he came out the winner. In that initial season Guy won 21 out of the 22 races he entered, becoming one of the most talked about drivers in the sport. He was designated national champion for that year. Thus a second successful career was launched at the age of forty while his first career as a bandleader was still in full swing.

He took a rest from speedboat racing until 1946 when he bought *Tempo VI*. Under its previous owner it had taken two Gold Cup victories and Lombardo drove it to its third when he entered the Champion circle of Gold Cup Winners in September 1946, a date that was high on his personal list of cherished accomplishments. That Gold Cup victory was all the sweeter since it was achieved before a crowd of more than 300,000 spectators. During the race he broke every record lap heat and drove the fastest ninety miles ever in a small power boat.

The following year he added more honors to his prestigious career in motorboat racing by taking the National Sweepstakes Regatta at Red Bank, New Jersey. On May 13, 1948, the man who had broken so many records on the water and on the bandstand set a new record of 119.7 miles per hour in a single engine hydro at Salton Sea, California. Before he gave up racing in the 1950's the indefatigable Guy had won every trophy in the United States, including the President's Cup and the Ford Memorial. He was national champion from 1946-1950. During that period, he achieved the same admiration and respect in racing circles that he had in the world of entertainment. An accident caused by floating debris during a race almost cost Guy his life, and it was then that Lilliebell put her foot down and persuaded her husband to end his racing days, but he remained active in the sport. He officiated at the Gold Cup, Presidential Cup and other national regattas. He was in the forefront of campaigns for safe boating and for the curtailment of unlimited hydroplane racing. Some of his best friends were killed in the unlimited events he was trying to help control. The baton notwithstanding, Guy's wistful eyes would follow the foam of boats on the water as millions followed him during his spectacular record-breaking "Tempo" era.

Above: Guy and Tempo VII racing at Bay City, Michigan, 1947.
Below: Guy receives trophy for winning that race as Lilliebell watches proudly.

Above, left to right: Carmen congratulates Guy on breaking the world's single-engine straightaway record at 119.7 miles per hour at Salton Sea, California, 1948.

Guy with Gar Wood, the racer he most admired, 1946.

Guy receives "Boating Man Of The Year" Trophy at 12th annual award banquet.

Guy and racing friend Jack Schaeffer, owner of "Such Cruise," Gull Lake, Michigan, 1949.

Bottom: Guy on Tempo after his world-shattering 119.7 MPH record for the single-engine hydro, 1948.

Bottom right: Guy with racing buddy, Jack Cooper (foreground), receiving speedboat "Hall of Fame" honors, New York, 1948.

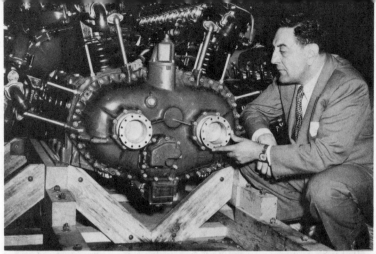

Above: Guy examines the high-powered and complicated engine of a new power driver for yet another Tempo.

Right: Fans get autographs from the national speedboat champion — or is it America's favorite bandleader?

Below: Guy takes time out to appear in boat race sequence in an episode of TV's "Route 66" in Tierra Verde, Florida.

Opposite page: Disneyland engagement in 1977 found Guy back to his boats — for a joyride this time.

Opposite page bottom: Guy relaxes in his Tempo commuter, 1972.

Above: Guy's first Tempo purchased for him by Lilliebell, 1929. It was custom-made and was turned over to them by former owner, who went broke in the stock market crash. The Lombardo home in background.
Below: Next Tempo, a 65 footer, and the Freeport, Long Island Lombardo home, 1955.

Above: *Guy in his Tempo yacht, a 45-foot express cruiser designed by John Hacker, used each evening as Guy commenced the Jones Beach performance.*
Below: *Guy in his Tempo runabout was a familiar sight during the summer on the Long Island waters.*

Political and Social Circles

Franklin Delano Roosevelt was Governor of New York when he was guest of honor at a special dinner on Long Island. The Lombardo orchestra, playing for the occasion, found itself confronted by the Governor.

"I like your music," he said simply.

"If you mean that, Governor," Guy said, smiling, "You'll invite us to play for you in Washington when you become President."

The Governor threw back his head in typical Rooseveltian manner and, laughing heartily, exclaimed, "You're on!"

He kept his word. The Lombardo band played at the inaugural ball in 1933, and this was the start of many appearances at inaugural balls in the future.

However, those balls were not the only appearances the band made in Washington. During FDR's initial term the band was flying to Washington to play for one official occasion or another, birthday parties for high officials, or receptions for distinguished foreign visitors.

On all these occasions, Guy would dutifully lead the band into the song everyone knew as the President's favorite, "Home on the Range." After several appearances, the President quietly drew Guy aside at one of these affairs and said, "I suppose you are going to play 'Home On The Range' again tonight?" He sighed with resignation. "Well, I guess you'll have to play the damn thing, just to continue the legend," he said, "but I really hate it."

After Vice President Harry S. Truman had succeeded Roosevelt to the presidency, Guy played the "Missouri Waltz" on a late-hour broadcast from the Roosevelt. Announcing the song he said, "And now here's President Truman's favorite song, 'The Missouri Waltz.' I don't suppose he's listening, but if he is, I hope he enjoys it."

A few minutes later the headwaiter came dashing up to the bandstand. The hotel had just received a telephone message from its Washington outlet, which had received a telephone call from the President of the United States himself! The President's message read, "Tell Mr. Lombardo I am listening and enjoyed 'Missouri Waltz' very much."

The President and Mrs. Eisenhower

request the pleasure of the company of

Mr. and Mrs. Lombardo

at dinner

on Tuesday, June 28, 1960

at eight o'clock

Guy joined other stars for F.D.R.'s 62nd birthday honors. Front from left: Louis Prima, Guy, Brian Aherne, Grantland Rice, Roland Young, Red Skelton, John Garfield, Meyer Davis, Walter Pidgeon, Brian Donlevy, Dean Murphy. Back: Joan Fontaine, Martha Scott, Mary Martin, Virginia Field, Mary Pickford, Mrs. Roosevelt, Lucille Ball, Maria Montez, Jinx Falkenburg, Jeanne Cagney, Lily Pons, Patricia Collinge.

Above: Guy presents trophy at Belmont Park Racetrack. That's Eddie Fisher on the right.

Left: Guy introduces Jinx Falkenburg and Robert Moses at his opening production at Jones Beach, 1954.

Below: Guy and actress, Sherry North, participate in a benefit for South Nassau Communities Hospital in Oceanside, Long Island, 1952.

In 1965, Guy and Count Basie played a joint concert in Miami Beach with Jackie Gleason directing.

The Lombardo orchestra also played for the inaugural of President Truman in 1949, and a warm relationship developed between them. One evening the band was playing a concert in Constitution Hall. Guy happened to look up at the Presidential Box and there was Mr. Truman, smiling happily. Guy had not known that the President was going to be there, and he confessed later that it made him a little nervous. At intermission the band went to the dressing room for a breather. After a couple of minutes, Guy started out the door and bumped into the President of the United States coming in.

"Mind if I come in and visit?" the President asked.

"Not at all, Mr. President, come right in," a startled Guy replied. While he looked for a chair, Truman calmly perched himself on the edge of a table. A brace of bodyguards had come in with him, but he dismissed them and turned his full attention to the men in the orchestra.

"I've always wanted to tell you how very flattered we were the time you called the radio station to tell them you were listening to us," Guy told him.

"Oh I always listen to you at that time of night," Truman said.

Somehow the conversation worked around to the number of receptions the President had to attend, and he began discussing the proper method of shaking hands.

"The trick is to do the squeezing yourself," he explained. "If you let your hand be squeezed it becomes mighty painful. Look, here's what I mean."

He reached out, grabbed Guy's hand, and gave it a firm squeeze. Then he demonstrated with Carmen, and Lebert. He jumped from the table and went around the room, grabbing each one's hand and shaking it.

The Lombardo orchestra also played at the inaugurals of both Eisenhower administrations. It may seem strange to political experts, but the Lombardos have given their personal political support to both Democrats and Republicans.

"We were all enthusiastic about President Roosevelt in his first two terms," Guy explained. "But I guess I'm just a born isolationist, and I didn't believe in Roosevelt's foreign policy. Then I was for General Eisenhower, but that doesn't make me a dyed-in-the-wool Republican. I'm for any man who can do the job."

Guy's appearances brought him into personal contact with many Presidents and their

Irving Berlin helped Guy celebrate his 20th wedding anniversary, 1949.

families. The Eisenhowers had Guy and the band play at White House functions and dinners. During one of the General's campaign tours, Guy and Carmen were found sharing the observation car of the Presidential touring train.

Another presidential story centers around New Year's Eve in 1972, when the Grand Ballroom of the Waldorf Astoria was overflowing with revellers who paid ninety dollars apiece, excluding liquor. At 12:30 a.m., New Year's Day, with an estimated 55,000,000 people watching and listening to the Royal Canadians throughout the United States, Canada, and overseas via satellite, the maitre d' rushed over to Lombardo's press agent and said, "The President is on the phone from the San Clemente White House and wants to talk to Guy while he's on television." Reacting quickly, the press agent countered, "It must be some nut. Hang up." The maitre d' persisted, but the publicist was just as persistent: "Either hang up or take the screwball's number and we'll call back." At 1:05 a.m., when the show went off the air, Lombardo took a ten-minute break, got the number from the maitre d' and returned the call, resulting in a five-minute conversation with President Nixon.

The Jimmy Carter inaugural in January 1977 found Guy Lombardo and the Royal Canadians once again invited to participate in the Washington activities. The band was designated to play at the Hilton Hotel ballroom. At the last minute Guy received a call from the President's son, Chip, informing him that the Carter family wanted Guy to switch to the Washington Armory, where the Georgia delegation and the Presidential family held sway. "But," Chip Carter admonished, "lets keep the switch quiet; we don't want everyone rushing to the Armory to dance to Guy Lombardo."

The Armory that night was filled with the usual glitter and excitement that comes with these victory calls. Then came the signal for Guy to play for the appearance of Vice President Walter Mondale and his wife. The Royal Canadians began their musical salute and the newly elected Vice President turned to Guy and said, "Guy, my wife said if we got on the same platform with Guy Lombardo and don't dance, she'll never speak to me again. So, Guy, how about a slow fox-trot?" Guy, with a happy smile, signaled the Royal Canadians to play a slow fox-trot, as the Vice President and his wife danced to the applause of the thousands of other guests at the Armory.

One hour later Guy was told that President

Above: Xavier Cugat and Abbe Lane visiting Guy at a Jones Beach show, choreographed by June Taylor, right, 1962.
Below: Walt Disney with Guy when he visited with him after seeing a Jones Beach show.

Carter and his wife Rosalynn were on their way into the Armory. The Georgia delegation whooped it up as Guy played "The Stars and Stripes Forever" requested by Mr. Carter himself.

The President made his way to the stage to shake hands with Guy, who then greeted Mrs. Carter. After the welcoming speech, Carter turned to Guy and said, "How about playing a song for Rosalynn and me. What do you suggest?" Guy, noticing that Mrs. Carter was wearing a blue gown, suggested "Red Roses for a Blue Lady." The President immediately countered with, "My lady is anything but blue tonight!" Lombardo settled the argument by directing the Royal Canadians into the strains of "Alice Blue Gown" as the newly elected Carters became the seventh President and first lady to listen and dance to the music of the Royal Canadians, while acknowledging the cheers of their inaugural celebrants.

As important to Guy as any of his appearances in Washington was the time Guy and Count Basie played a joint concert atop the Doral

Above: *Tony Randall joins Guy, Lebert and Carmen during the Royal Canadians' record-breaking engagement at the Riverboat in New York City.*
Below: *Lionel Hampton congratulates Guy during the band's Riverboat engagement.*

Beach Hotel in Miami Beach in 1964. It was the height of the winter season and while Basie's band was playing downstairs, the Royal Canadians were working on the Starlight Roof. The bands were merged for a one-time only bash, with press and celebrities to be the guests of the hotel. The crowd which overflowed the room caused a monumental jam-up and a delay of at least an hour in the starting time.

Basie's band was to play from Lombardo's charts. Lombardo's crew would play from Basie's. Then they'd join forces under the baton of Jackie Gleason. Believe it or not, it worked! The Count's musicians may have seemed a bit uncomfortable with Lombardo's music but when the Royal Canadians attacked the Basie charts, you could close your eyes and not know who was playing.

Lombardo recalled that gala event very well. "I always told everyone my musicians were the best; they sure believed me that night! A raft of singers joined with each of our bands and Jackie Gleason had a field day conducting our massed musicians. it was a night none of us will ever forget."

The Lombardo band has also played for countless foreign dignitaries. At times Guy had to go beyond the call of duty, as on the occasion when the late Emperor Haile Selassie of Ethiopia asked him to take a stroll along the boardwalk at Jones Beach. Though Guy was trim and athletic, walking was not his favorite exercise. The Emperor, however, insisted on covering every inch of the boardwalk. Finally, Guy just couldn't take it anymore. Up ahead he saw a comfortable bench.

"Please," he said to the interpreter who was accompanying them, "Would you explain to His Highness that I just can't walk another inch and would greatly appreciate it if we could sit down for a while?"

The interpreter interpreted. The Emperor smiled kindly and said something and the interpreter translated: "His Highness says, please sit down. He'll stroll around until you're ready to walk again." That's what the Emperor did, too. When Guy was rested, they walked back together.

Two of the greatest thrills the Lombardos had were playing for the Commonwealth Balls held in New York, first on the occasion of the official visit to America of the Queen Mother,

then for Her Majesty, Queen Elizabeth.

Every man in the orchestra remembers one particular moment during the ball honoring the Queen Mother. As she passed in front of the orchestra, she smiled. The magic of her gracious personality gave the impression to Guy and every member of the band that she was smiling expressly at him.

The second Commonwealth Ball, again held in the Seventh Regiment Armory on Park Avenue, honored Queen Elizabeth and Prince Philip. Guy Lombardo and the Royal Canadians were invited to play at the specific request of the Queen. The orchestra was on tour in the Midwest at the time, and in order to play for the ball a number of engagements had to be cancelled. Guy flew the band back to New York. Without a doubt, all of the members of the orchestra agreed this was the most dignified, beautiful dance for which they had ever played. It was truly one of the highlights of their career.

"After the dance was over," Guy later related, "the Queen and Prince Philip met with half a dozen people or so, including Mayor Wagner of New York, in a small room off the ballroom. I was honored to be invited. Prince Philip was the center of the conversation. He talked about the different styles of popular music, and he knew what he was talking about. He told me he knew our band well. He had several of our records at the Palace and played them regularly.

"Then the Prince directed his conversation to someone else and I stepped back to get a glass of punch. As I turned, I suddenly found myself standing face to face with Queen Elizabeth. I was utterly flabbergasted. I'm not usually at a loss for words, but I was speechless. Here was the Queen of the British Empire, this beautiful woman, with the warmest, sweetest smile on her face, and I couldn't say a word. Finally I recovered enough to return her smile. I know this sounds presumptuous, but I had the feeling that even Queens could be lonely, but before I could speak, she smiled again, turned, and walked to a nearby chair and sat down, all alone."

Few orchestra leaders would be equally at home at the Commonwealth Ball and the World Series, but then few orchestra leaders are Guy Lombardo. For years he was known as "Mr. World Series." It all dated back to the days when the late Dan Topping, who was to become the owner of the New York Yankees, was one of the young people who danced regularly at the Roosevelt Grill. When Topping acquired the Yankees, and the Yankees acquired the pennant, Topping asked Guy to play at the World Series. He played many opening games for Yankees' series openers since then, as well as participating musically at the "Old Timers'" game.

The procedure for these baseball game appearances was routine to Guy's band. They played at the beginning of the game, of course. The musicians took up their positions in center field facing homeplate. The band played a half-hour concert, while the teams had their warm-up practice. Then the band played the "Star Spangled Banner" while the flag was raised. As the managers gave the umpires their line-up for the game, the pianos and chairs were removed from the field.

The band traveled long distances to play the Series. In 1963, for instance, the day before the World Series opened, the band was in Sioux Falls, South Dakota. They played an engagement there that night and at 1:30 a.m. boarded a chartered plane for Omaha. There they picked up a regularly scheduled flight to Chicago where they changed again for a plane to Idlewild (now Kennedy International) in New York. A bus was waiting to take them to Yankee Stadium. The tickets Guy had bought for the game did the band little good, for not one man saw a single pitch. Instead, they returned to the airport immediately after their concert at the stadium, flew to Chicago, changed there for Minneapolis, and in Minneapolis boarded their regular bus (which had dead-headed from Sioux Falls) for La Crosse, Wisconsin. They arrived at 8:30 p.m. and played 9 p.m. to 1 a.m. Thus, in the space of twenty-four hours, the Royal Canadians had played the "sweetest music" in Sioux Falls, South Dakota, Yankee Stadium, New York and La Crosse, Wisconsin.

Six months later in April of 1964, the Lombardos were back in New York playing for a baseball game, but not in Yankee Stadium. The upstart Mets, the new National League team which was going all out to compete with their wealthy rivals from the Bronx, hired the Lombardo Band to play for their opening game!

Guy has a reunion with his 100-year old godmother, Mrs. Mary Davis, in Toronto, Canada.

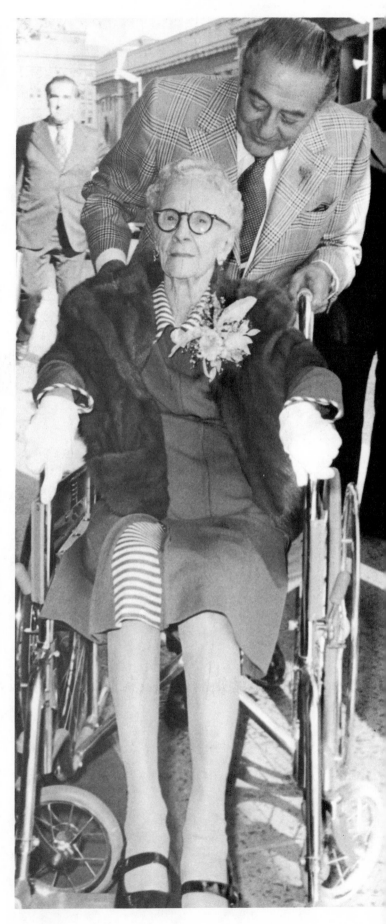

145

Above: *Tommy Henrich, Guy, and Bob Feller at Yankee Stadium "Old Timers' Day" game, 1968.*
Guy and the band played at many N.Y. Yankees baseball games, and were considered good luck for the team.
Left: *At Yankee Stadium, Bobby Thompson tries his hand at bandleading. (He went back to baseball.)*
Opposite page, top: *Sports announcer Don Dunphy interviews Guy during a televised regatta.*
Opposite page, bottom: *Yankees Ralph Houk and Yogi Berra receive the first recording from Guy of the Royal Canadians' version of the Yankees' official song.*

Right: Guy greets world's surfing champ, Felipe Pomar, when the Peruvian athlete visits Jones Beach, 1968.
Below: Guy with some Indianapolis friends at the Speedway before the annual "500." Lebert is at left.

Left: Thanks to Dr. Michael DeBakey, Guy was up and around soon after surgery at Houston Methodist Hospital, 1967.
Below: Guy and Jules Stein at Universal studios, 1974. Jules Stein founded the Music Corporation of America and represented the Royal Canadians for many years. He brought them to New York in 1929.

Above: *Perry Como and Carmen applaud Guy's speech at the opening of a new arena in Hempstead, Long Island, 1948.*
Below: *Guy and Al Quodbach, who gave the Lombardos their start in Chicago at his Granada Cafe.*

Above: *Martha Raye cuts up with Guy during a Jones Beach visit.*
Below: *Frank Sinatra, Vaughn Monroe, and Guy in the mid-forties.*

Above: Guy and friend Morton Downey renew old times at a dinner get-together.
Below: Guy applauds Ella Logan as she is introduced to the audience during a visit to the Roosevelt Hotel, 1954.

Above: Guy and Helen O'Connell, who appeared on several New Years' Eve Lombardo
Below: Guy, Helen O'Connell, and William Gargan backstage at the Riviera Hotel in Las Vegas, where the Royal Canadians performed many engagements.

Best Wishes
Guy Lombardo

When Success Almost Went To Their Heads

With the tremendous success of the band at the Granada Cafe in Chicago came pressures, pleasures, offers for appearances—and dangers. The dangers derived from the number of celebrities and famous musicians who crowded the Granada to listen to the Lombardo sound. Trying to fathom the band's sudden popularity and its smashing acceptance by a dancing, adoring public of both young and old was a challenge. Name bandleaders and their sidemen would push into the Granada, listen, and then whisper to one another, "What the hell is going on?" "Do you catch anything that I don't?" "What in the world is the secret of these kids from Canada?" "It's too simple a beat, too simple an arrangement, it sounds too easy on the ear."

Of course that *was* the secret. The way the Lombardos did it, it *was* easy. They played the melody with only the simplest embellishments so you could recognize it at once. They weren't playing for musicians who came to listen with trained ears, but for people who wanted to hear the melody of their favorite songs and dance to a beat they could understand.

The criticism of the musicians on the outside somewhat endangered the new-found success of the Lombardo orchestra. The members of the band began to have doubts about themselves. Performers are sensitive and impressionable human beings and the Royal Canadians are no exception. They began having second thoughts and misgivings about what other musicians thought of them. Now that they had reached the stage of playing for the great names in the entertainment world, they asked themselves: Were they playing well enough? Shouldn't they play more sophisticated arrangements? Shouldn't the individual members attempt to achieve a more virtuoso performance?

Lebert, always the most sensitive and impressionable member of the group, was particularly plagued by self-doubt and worry. He knew his own limitations, and whenever a recognized musical figure happened to be in the room he became self-conscious and nervous. One night in Cleveland, for example, Vincent Lopez had come to hear the orchestra play and Lebert had tightened up to the point where he actually missed a few notes. Now, in Chicago, it was worse than ever. Hardly a night went by that there wasn't somebody famous at the Granada, listening to the band with a critical ear. One evening Lebert looked up to see Paul Whiteman, who had achieved phenomenal success in the entertainment world while the Lombardos were still teenagers in London, seated at a table. Beads of sweat popped out on Lebert's forehead.

Louie Panico came in regularly and, whenever he did, Lebert became extremely uncomfortable. Panico had been his inspiration and model, but now Lebert was one-third owner and sole trumpeter of an orchestra far more famous than the one in which Louie Panico was just a sideman. It didn't seem fair. But for Lebert the worst of all was the night the immortal Bill Biederbecke came in. Bix was then at the height of his glory. Playing with the Paul Whiteman band, he had brought something new to popular music. While Bix was in the Granada, Lebert was in agony.

It was then that Lebert Lombardo, first and only trumpet for the orchestra that was the rage of Chicago, began taking trumpet lessons on the sly in an effort to develop a "legitimate tone" and sound just like that of a thousand other trumpet players. The vibrato which was so vital to the Lombardo sound began to fade away. Guy picked up the difference immediately. Although he would have had difficulty playing two notes on a trumpet, Guy's ear could detect the slightest difference in any instrument. In fact when Lebe sometimes changed his regular trumpet for another one, Guy could spot it at once. He knew something was amiss.

"Are you using a different trumpet?" Guy asked Lebert. "You sound like you're blowing through a gaspipe."

"No, no," Lebe exclaimed.

"Then you must have a new mouthpiece," Guy responded. Again, Lebe demurred.

"I'm not doing anything different," he said.

Lebe was a novice at fibbing, and his poor attempt at lying was obvious to Guy. Lebe finally admitted that he'd been taking lessons. Guy raised his hand in utter amazement. "My God!" he shouted. "Any trumpet player in the country would give his right arm to be where you are sitting and you want to change! If you go near that teacher again, I'll straighten out that trumpet and wrap it around your neck!"

But the pressure to change for the sake of change, to do things differently under the guise of improvement, was too strong to resist. It even spread to Guy. After the smashing success of that first season in Chicago, the Lombardos got together and decided that for the second season they'd really outdo themselves. Success had come too easy for them; now they were going to work for it.

"Oh, we're really going to knock 'em dead this year," Guy said. For several weeks they worked like beavers putting together new arrangements to replace the old ones. Though they didn't bring in a professional arranger, they did ask a fine musician they had known in Cleveland, Boyd Bunch, to come in and write down the new passages they created.

The sky was the limit. Out went the famous saxophones with the identifying vibrato; in came clarinets played straight. Out went Lebe's famous mute; in came the standard tone. Other changes were made throughout the orchestra. Then the season began. They played their wonderful new arrangements, sat back, and waited for the usual avalanche of fan mail, packed houses, and adulation. None was forthcoming. The fan mail dropped off sharply. In addition to this concrete evidence that things were not as they used to be, Guy and the boys in the band themselves felt, even as they were playing, that

LEONARDO

Reprinted by permission of the artist.

Above: *The sound of Lebert Lombardo's trumpet is one of the reasons for the continuing success of The Royal Canadians.*

something was wrong, But what? They couldn't figure it out. Or perhaps they refused to recognize what subconsciously they all knew.

As time went by, the Lombardos saw success blowing up before their eyes. Panic set in. But just at this time fate once again intervened. Guy stopped by a local barbershop for a quick trim before the evening show. The barber, Louis Messini, was one of the band's biggest fans. Whenever Guy, Carmen, or Lebe came in, Louie would tell how he and his wife had listened to the boys the night before and how wonderful it was. But on this particular morning, Louie, instead of giving out his usual extravagant praise, inquired tentatively, "Say, you must have changed some of the boys in the band, huh?"

Many a man seeing success collapse about him like a house of cards might well have brushed aside such a remark. Guy, however, courteously replied that the personnel was still the same.

"That's funny," Louie went on, "my wife and I were listening to you last night and it just didn't seem the same somehow."

Guy shot the barber a quick look, "What do you mean? How does it seem different ?"

Lou took a step back. "Don't get me wrong, Mr. Lombardo," he said. "I don't know anything about music; I'm no musician, so maybe I shouldn't be talking."

"You go right ahead and talk," Guy said, putting him at ease. "One of the reasons I'm listening to you is that you're not a musician."

All Lou could do, however, was reiterate the fact that the band didn't sound the way it used to, and from the tone of his voice Guy quickly judged that to Lou, the barber, it didn't sound as good as before. Early the next morning, Guy went directly to radio station WBBM.

"I'd like to take a look at all the old logs of our programs," Guy said. "I want to see what we

So, Guy had a complete list of every song he had played on every program. He spent the entire day in the WBBM offices. Out of his study a pattern began to emerge. For one thing, checking on Les Atlas' comment on the bump-bah, bump-bah, he found program after program in which the famous schottische rhythm didn't appear even once. Previously, when going from a slow ballad to a fast tune, for example, they'd make the transition by playing a song in a schottische rhythm in between. It not only tended to minimize the sudden contrast, but the rhythm was pleasant in its own right. Now they were neglecting it completely.

Other facts emerged from Guy's study of these programs. Somehow or other, reading the titles on paper and thinking back over the way the band played them, he began to realize the great changes that had taken place in the style and sound of the band. In his mind's ear he detected that Lebe's delightful muted trumpet was missing completely from the current arrangements. In his imagination he listened in vain for that inimitable vibrato of Carmen's and the saxes, so expressive of the feeling that Carm had always put into a song. That was lacking too.

Late in the afternoon Guy Lombardo came to full realization of what he had done. As he explained it later, "The very things that people liked about our music were what we had deliberately thrown away! I hurried back to discuss the matter with Carm and Lebe. It didn't take long to make them see it too. The very first thing we did was take those smarty-pants arrangements we'd worked on for so long and throw them in the trash can. We went back to the tried-and-true Lombardo style that had put us on top at the very beginning."

So, thanks to a friendly barber and Guy's willingness to listen to him tell the Lombardos how to run a band, they got back on the right track. Many years later Guy looked back at that episode with a feeling of deep thankfulness that he and the band learned their lesson early in their career, when it was possible to correct their mistakes quickly, and to profit by it. The history of entertainment in the past few decades is rife with examples of bands that were not so lucky, who got off the track and never got back on again. A well-known example is Paul Whiteman's great dance band of the early 1920's, which went on a symphonic kick and never completely regained its popular audience. Another example was Shep Fields, who burst onto the national scene in the 1930's with a delightful sound he called "rippling rhythm." The Lombardos, both fans and friends of Fields, urged him to stick with "rippling rhythm," but Shep got away from it and his great popularity decreased from then on.

played before, and what we're playing now."

"Okay," agreed WBBM manager Les Atlas, "I'll get 'em for you, but why do you want to look at them?"

"I don't know myself," Guy said. "People say we sound different this year and I want to figure out the reason."

"You want my opinion?" Atlas asked.

"I sure do," Guy replied.

"You're not going bump-bah, bump-bah, the way you used to," Atlas said.

"Bump-bah, bump-bah?" Guy asked.

"Yeah, you know, like in 'Button Up Your Overcoat' — bump-bah, bump-bah."

"I think I see what you mean," Guy whispered.

He sat down with the program logs. At that point in the history of radio it was very important for every station to keep an exact log of what was played at the time. It was a great national game to see how many stations your set would pick up, but just listening to them wasn't enough; you had to have proof with an "echo stamp." If you sent WBBM a self-addressed card saying, "I heard Guy Lombardo playing 'Button Up Your Overcoat' at 11:22 p.m., January 28, 1928," the station would check the log, stamp your card, and mail it back to you.

Kay Kayser

Bob Crosby

The bandleader fraternity was a close-knit family. Guy enjoyed their company at the Roosevelt Hotel or at his East Point restaurant.

Opposite Page: *Guy with Fred Waring and Mitchell Ayres.*

Freddy Martin

Artie Shaw

Eddy Duchin

Benny Goodman

Vincent Lopez

Vaughan Monroe

Left: *Benny Strong, Tommy Dorsey, Sammy Kaye, Guy, Shep Fields, and Vincent Lopez drop in at the Roosevelt Grill for a baton-wavers' holiday.*

Over the years an integral part of the Lombardo philosophy and success was Guy's insistence on sticking to what the band does best. He thought this whole matter out, and he knew what he was doing.

Though the band occasionally tried other novel approaches, such as calypso and country and western music, its success has always been predicated on its set style. "We have never really changed," Guy pointed out. "We've improved, yes, but we've never changed."

Indeed, the band today has the same businesslike approach to everything it does. It has seldom shortened its rehearsal schedule, never diminished its pride in its work. It is one of the most professional bands in the business. The members arrive at each date with their complete library, and each man carries in, and is responsible for, his own work. They work very hard on each performance, and insist that everything comes out right. Sometimes at recordings, Guy worked in the control room, but it seemed that when he was in front of his band, waving his hand, the men played better. As soon as they're finished, each man picks up his own music and his own instruments, and out they go. Though others may not have imitated the band's personal

habits, numerous bands imitated its style.

What caused it all to happen in the first place? Lombardo explained it this way: "Bands happened," he said, "musicians happened, and we happened."

The phrase "popular music" draws different emphasis from different people. Guy liked to dwell on the first word. "History has proven," he said, "that we have been important innovators and that we have created more styles and sold more records than any other band."

"But," he went on, "there are audiences for all styles. I think rock and Dixieland and opera and symphony styles are all great, and there has always been enough for everyone's taste. Bing Crosby may not be in a class with Jan Peerce, but he has more showmanship. That doesn't mean they have to be compared.

"I try to put myself in the listener's seat," he explained. "I try to hear what the people listening to us hear. Today when a new song is brought in, I don't even look at what our arrangers have done with it. I don't want to be familiar with it. I don't want to anticipate what's coming. I want to listen to it the way the average fan listens to it, just as a pretty piece of music.

"Take a technical thing like a musical chord.

160

Sometimes a chord can be perfectly correct in a strictly musical sense, but it just doesn't sound good to my ear. When that happens the chord is out. I don't care how correct it may be musically.

"I don't countenance any of that way-out, progressive type jazz in our music. Sure, it's wonderful for those who understand it, but there are not enough of those people to go around. When I travel all over America and look at the farmhouses and the small settlements and the split-level suburbs, I ask myself, 'Do these people appreciate G-ninth chords, F-sixth chords? Do they want flatted fifths?' I don't think they do.

"Stan Kenton, whom I respect, but disagree with, says that he wants to educate people. Once, when he took his band on tour, he said that if anybody danced to his music he'd consider himself a failure. Well, education may be fine for Stan but not for us. The Lombardo band is not in the education business. We're in the entertainment business. When people come out to see us in person, or sit down at the end of a long day and put on a Lombardo record on the stereo, they're going to get melodies that they can listen to with pleasure and appreciation. If you want to call it corny, go ahead. But I can tell you right now that we're going to keep on playing not for your education, but for your enjoyment, and we don't contemplate changing, not for one moment."

There was one other occasion, however, when the band almost went astray in the Windy City. Back on the right track, the Royal Canadians had again become the craze of Chicago. The Palace Theatre, a famed Chicago vaudeville house, offered Guy a week's engagement at what at that time was a whopping rate of $4,000. The boys got together to discuss the kind of show they would put on. The consensus was that in a vaudeville theatre they'd better put on a vaudeville show. After all, people could hardly be expected to pay an admission price to sit in a theatre seat and listen to dance music.

So, with great enthusiasm they dragged out the big bag of costumes and effects known affectionately as the "bag of jewels," and began working up a program that would have the Palace customers rolling in the aisles. Derf Higman of course would put on his harness and blinders for "Thanks for the Buggy Ride," and naturally he would eat a great big sandwich for "A Cup of Coffee and a Sandwich and You." There was

Louis Prima, who Guy heard in New Orleans in 1934 and brought to New York where he became an immediate success.

much more of the same: corny-looking gowns, old lampshades for hats, and all the other accoutrements that went with the so-called novelty number.

Opening night arrived and the boys outdid themselves. Never have such capers been seen on stage. When the curtain came down they walked off, pleased as punch, straight into the outraged bellow of an apoplectic theatre manager. "What in the hell is the matter with you guys?" he roared. "Who told you you were comedians? If I'd wanted comedians, I'd have hired comedians. For four thousands bucks I want music, not trash!"

Through one of the coincidences that shape entertainment history, the leading Chicago critic of the day, Ashton Stevens of the *Herald and Examiner*, missed the first performance and attended, instead, the second. He was spared the novelty numbers and heard a full program of beautiful Lombardo music. He went back to his paper to write a glowing review in which he referred to the band as "The softest and sweetest jazzmen on any stage this side of heaven." His words caught on, changed slightly in context, but not in meaning; they have been used ever since to describe the strains of the Lombardo orchestra as "the sweetest music this side of heaven."

Rehearsals for the Royal Canadians were serious with no nonsense tolerated by Guy.

ANNIE DOESN'T LIVE HERE ANYMORE

INTRODUCED AND FEATURED BY

GUY LOMBARDO

LYRIC BY
JOE YOUNG AND JOHNNY BURKE
MUSIC BY
HAROLD SPINA

Irving Berlin, Inc.
MUSIC PUBLISHERS
1607 Broadway   New York

There's A Story Behind Every Melody

John Wilson, the highly respected and nationally acclaimed jazz critic and authority, whose columns in *The New York Times* are read avidly by many enthusiastic followers, once interviewed Lombardo for *Reader's Digest*. He learned from Guy that there was a story behind many of the tunes recorded by the Royal Canadians. The following are some of Guy's favorite musical reminiscences and the stories behind some of the many numbers recorded by him throughout the years of the Lombardo disc delvings.

"The Blue Skirt Waltz"

This haunting Czech waltz is a tune that Guy Lombardo tried not to record. Guy had great respect for the judgement of Jack Kapp, head of Decca Records, but when Kapp suggested this waltz, Guy turned it down as "too commercial." Kapp insisted, however, and when Guy eventually agreed, he found himself with a tremendous hit. Recorded in 1948, "The Blue Skirt Waltz" is still the band's biggest request whenever they play in the Midwest.

"A Sailboat in the Moonlight"

One evening in the Freeport, Long Island harbor, Guy and Carmen were sitting for the first time on Guy's brand new fifty-five foot boat. "It was a thrilling evening for me," Guy remembered, and it must have been an equally thrilling time for a young couple who passed close by in a sailboat. Said Guy: "Isn't that romantic, those two kids on a sailboat in the moonlight." Whereupon in true MGM-musical style, Carmen exclaimed: "Wouldn't that make a wonderful song title!" Together, he and close friend, John Jacob Loeb, wrote the song. But what Guy remembered most was, "Here is Carmen thinking of a romantic song title and I'm practically making love to my new fifty-five foot boat!"

"Midnight in Moscow"

Lebert, who plays the trumpet solo in this adaptation of a Russian song, was the band's drummer back in London, Ontario. But at sixteen he fell in love with the muted trumpet style of Louis Panico, a star in Isham Jones' band in the early twenties. When Lebert had mastered some of Panico's solos, Guy would occasionally let him play one. Lebert played them holding his trumpet with one hand and drumming with the other. Then one night Guy fired the band's trumpet player for yawning on the stand. Lebert was moved from drums to trumpet and has been the band's only trumpet ever since.

"I'll See You in My Dreams"

"This is my favorite song," said Guy. "For me, it's the perfect wedding of words and music. I heard it when we first went to Cleveland. Isham Jones, who wrote it, recorded it for Brunswick. We got a sample record. It was Sunday afternoon, and we all went up to the apartment with our girls. We put on this record and I cried and I cried and I cried. I thought it was the prettiest music I'd ever heard in my life."

"Canadian Capers"

An echo of the ragtime era, this lively tune is one of the most popular of the Twin Piano pieces played by Fred Kreitzer, the Lombardos' original pianist, and Francis Vigneau, the band's first second-pianist. Despite the fact that the Lombardos were born in London, Ontario, and have always called their band the Royal Canadians, Guy did not choose this tune because of any implied connection with Canada. He learned to be careful about that when the Canadian Broadcasting Corporation began picking up his annual New Year's Eve broadcast and asked him to include something Canadian in it. Guy was obliging. "And now for our Canadian viewers," he said one New Year's Eve, "here is 'Maple Leaf Rag'." It was not until several years later that he found that the tune was named not for Canada's national symbol but for a saloon in Sedalia, Missouri, the Maple Leaf Club, where Scott Joplin composed it!

"Hop Scotch Polka"

Guy Lombardo remembered that "a little Englishman came over to the Roosevelt Hotel" to interest Guy in his song, "Hop-Scotch Polka." The "little Englishman" was Billy Whitlock, a British vaudeville performer, who had adapted "Hop-Scotch Polka" from a traditional folk song, either Irish or Scottish. He originally called it "Scotch Hot" when he introduced it in English music halls, but it became a polka for American audiences.

"You're Driving Me Crazy"

Walter Donaldson, one of the most successful songwriters of the late twenties ("At Sundown," "My Blue Heaven," "Carolina in the Morning") was, despite his success, constantly broke because of his profligate spending habits. But he was an ingenious conniver when it came to raising funds. He called Guy at 7 a.m. one morning in 1930 to tell him he had just finished a song. Would Guy, who was such a close friend that he was paying Donaldson's room rent, put it on the air that night? An arrangement was quickly put together which the band played that night and every night for a week. Within three days Donaldson's publishers were besieged with orders for the sheet music. But they could not publish the song because they did not have the verse and Donaldson had deliberately disappeared. Three days later Donaldson reemerged. "I've got the verse," he told his publisher, "but I need $10,000." The publisher, Guy recalled, had to get a loan from the bank. "Walter was such a conniver," Guy said with an appreciative twinkle, "that he arranged the whole thing so that we'd introduce the song, create the demand, and then he'd go ask for the money."

WALTER DONALDSON

"Dancing in the Dark"

In the winter of 1930-31 the Royal Canadians were playing their second season at the Roosevelt Grill in New York City. One night Arthur Schwartz and Howard Dietz, the songwriters who had composed "Something to Remember You By," commented on the changing lighting effects in the room. Guy showed them how he could regulate the lights from the bandstand. "People seem to enjoy dancing in the dark," Guy told them, dimming the lights to demonstrate. "A few nights later," Guy recalled, "they came back and said, 'You gave us a good idea for a song'." That song was "Dancing in the Dark." Although written for the 1931 revue *The Band Wagon*, it was played for the first time by Guy and The Royal Canadians at the Roosevelt Grill, with the lights dimmed, of course.

"Get Out Those Old Records"

This is sheer nostalgia, evoking memories not only of those old records of the twenties and thirties in general (the record came out in 1950), but of the Lombardo records in particular. The countermelody is sung by Carmen Lombardo who wrote the song. But by 1950 he had turned most of the vocal chores over to Kenny Gardner, who had been discovered singing on radio in 1941 by the Lombardos' sister, Elaine. Kenny then joined the band, but almost immediately went off to war. By the time he returned to the band in 1946, he had married Elaine and was part of the Lombardo family.

"Who?"

The Lombardos have been playing Jerome Kern's "Who?" since 1925, when the song first appeared in the musical *Sunny* and the Lombardo band was beginning to acquire some local fame in Canada. Guy was originally attracted to "Who?" by the famous recording made by George Olsen and His Music. This was the record that "made" the Olsen band. "Olsen came in with a soft-singing trio that we probably copied a little bit," says Guy with a chuckle. "We thought that 'Who?' by George Olsen was the greatest thing that ever happened; but instead of doing the vocal like he did, we did it as an instrumental." Originally it was a regular full-band instrumental, but in recent years it has become a feature for the Twin Pianos.

"Seems Like Old Times"

This mixture of nostalgia and happiness, reflecting the national mood in 1946 when World War II had ended, is the only song that Guy himself helped write. Carmen and John Jacob Loeb wrote it as a lively piece with a sarcastic attitude about getting the runaround. "You're still fooling around with somebody else, seems like old times." "They were trying to rewrite 'Goody, Goody'," says Guy. "I told them they were getting the wrong feeling. I shifted some of the lyrics, moved 'Dinner dates at seven ...' from the bottom to the top, took out the sarcasm and changed the tempo. We slowed it down and it became an overnight smash." Arthur Godfrey heard it a few days after the record was released and started playing it so often on his radio show that it became his theme.

"Bill Bailey, Won't You Please Come Home?"

When a band has been popular for almost half a century, as the Lombardo band has been, its repertoire eventually becomes a fascinating collection of Americana. The Lombardo repertoire has grown in two basic ways: through creating or playing the big pop hits of the moment and through finding material for albums built around a specific idea. The band has made several albums based on the "songs that everybody sings" approach, albums that have started them playing a number of songs they might not have thought suited to their style. "Bill Bailey," originally recorded for such an album, has become one of the greatest favorites at Lombardo dances where it literally is a song that everybody sings."

"Annie Doesn't Live Here Anymore"

During the 1930's Guy and Carmen often asked publishers to send them their reject songs in which no one had shown any interest. While the band was playing at the World's Fair in Chicago in 1933, the two brothers spent an afternoon going through some rejects and came across "Annie Doesn't Live Here Anymore." Guy couldn't decide if it was supposed to be a funny song ("some city dude has taken Annie away from him") or a sad song ("the undertaker took her away"). But Carmen was convinced it would be a hit; so Guy called the publisher and said the Lombardos would introduce the song if they could have a six-week exclusive on it. "Six weeks?" exclaimed the surprised publisher. "You can have six years." It was a hit in less than six weeks but Guy still didn't know whether it was a sad song or a funny one.

"St. Louis Blues"

This, one of the earliest Lombardo hits, originated when the band was in Cleveland in 1927. It became famous for Carmen's dazzlingly long clarinet note ("Hold it, Carmen!") and the unusual lyrics, which replace the originals by W.C. Handy. Lebert Lombardo, the trumpet-playing brother, heard a black trumpet player in Cleveland singing them and paid him $5 to write them down. Lebert never knew the trumpet player's name or where he got the lyrics. He had disappeared by the time the lyrics had helped make "St. Louis Blues" a Lombardo hit.

"Auld Lang Syne"

The Lombardos were already ending their dance engagements with "Auld Lang Syne" when they were still teenagers in Canada. The area around London, Ontario, was Scottish, and it was traditional there to play "Auld Lang Syne" at the end of an evening. When the band was engaged for the Robert Burns Panatella radio show in the fall of 1929, Guy decided "Auld Lang Syne" would be an appropriate theme, since burns wrote the song. They used "Comin' through the Rye" as the opener. A few months later, when the Royal Canadians played their first double-network New Year's Eve program, signing off on CBS just before midnight and beginning NBC right after midnight, they used "Auld Lang Syne" to bridge the gap. By then it had become so closely associated with the band that it became its permanent theme.

"Always"

Irving Berlin's lovely waltz has been in the Royal Canadians' repertoire since, as Guy says, "we were cutting our eye-teeth in Cleveland. That was one of the tunes we were playing at the Claremont when Louis Bleet kept saying, 'Play soft, play the medleys.'" Berlin wrote "Always" in 1925 while he was courting the socially prominent Ellin Mackay. When they were married in 1926, Berlin gave his wife all the rights to the song, a wedding present that within twenty years had produced more than $60,000 in royalties.

CARMEN LOMBARDO and KENNY GARDNER

"Stars Fell on Alabama"

When the Royal Canadians introduced this song in 1934, Carmen Lombardo sang it. Its lyrics brought out all the "eccentricities" that some satirized in Carmen's singing, the hard, rolling r's in *stars, arms, drama*, and the precise full value given to every consonant and syllable. This diction had been drilled into all the Lombardo boys by their mother and their sister Elaine, both of whom were sticklers for clear, clean enunciation. When Kenny Gardner succeeded Carmen as vocalist he softened these mannerisms a bit; but they are still recognizably present, possibly because Kenny Gardner is married to Elaine.

"Easter Parade"

Around 1930 Irving Berlin had a writing block. The most successful and prolific American songwriter no longer was able to compose a song. At this time the Lombardos were picking hit after hit on their radio show, so Berlin asked to sit behind the band at the Roosevelt Hotel to get the feeling of this music that appealed to "the kids." After two weeks he went home to write some songs and offered two to Guy to introduce. The Lombardos made one of them the "Hit of the Week" on their radio show. An hour later a discouraged Berlin called and said, "Thanks, Guy, but that's the worst song I ever heard." Several months later the Lombardo band, enroute to California, heard a trio in Philadelphia playing a lovely melody. What was it? It was from Irving Berlin's new show, *Easter Parade*, they were told. When they got to Los Angeles, the Lombardos introduced the song and became better known for it there than for "Auld Lang Syne."

IRVING BERLIN

"Coquette"

When the Lombardos first arrived in Chicago in 1927, Carmen had a melody running through his head looking for lyrics. While the band was in Cleveland, it had plugged many songs by Gus Kahn, a fabulously successful lyricist, so Carmen had the temerity to approach Kahn about writing some lyrics. This involved getting up at 6:00 a.m. to meet Kahn at a golf course at 7:30 and follow him around the course (Carmen did not play golf). But one night Kahn called to say he had just been to New York and had seen Helen Hayes in her big hit, *Coquette*. He had lyrics, which he dictated over the phone. Two nights later the Lombardo band went on the air for the first time and introduced "Coquette," the song that became their first hit and their first record for Columbia, a best seller.

"Hawaiian Wedding Song"

When the Royal Canadians are on tour, each musician carries about two hundred arrangements with him. During the thirty-three years that the band played every winter at the Roosevelt Hotel in New York, a room in back of the bandstand was filled with arrangements, "Stacks and stacks of them," says Guy. In this collection, there were more arrangements of "Hawaiian Wedding Song" than any other tune. "We'd make an arrangement, put it in the books, and forget about it," Guy explains. "Then the parts would get lost. So we'd have a new one made, put it in the books, and those parts would get lost. Then I'd call it out some night, and everyone would be playing a different orchestration."

"Doll Dance"

"Doll Dance" has been a piano feature in the Lombardo band ever since it was first heard in 1927 in Carter De Haven's *Music Box Revue* at the Music Box Theatre in Hollywood. That was the year that the Royal Canadians moved from Cleveland to Chicago, where "Doll Dance" became the band's big piano number. It is still emulated today when the Twin Pianos hold forth.

"I'm Forever Blowing Bubbles"

Most of the singing in the Lombardo orchestra is by a soloist or by The Lombardo Trio. The Lombardo Sextet, heard on this waltz, was made possible by the fact that in the late forties the band was loaded with instrumentalists who could sing. In addition to Carmen and Kenny Gardner, there were, among others, Cliff Grass and Freddie Higman in the saxophone section (they were two thirds of the Lombardo Trio) and Don Rodney on guitar. So, when an arrangement such as this called for a choir effect, six band members dropped their instruments and stood up to sing.

"Down among the Sheltering Palms"

The instrumental sounds most closely identified with the Royal Canadians are Carmen's smooth alto saxophone and Lebert's crisp, relaxed trumpet. But a third Lombardo sound came into the band in the 1930's when 19-year old brother Victor joined up, playing baritone saxophone. At first he was a relatively anonymous member of the saxophone section but, later switching to soprano sax, he played occasional solos such as the one in the last chorus of this World War I tune.

"Bell Bottom Trousers"

"Bell Bottom Trousers" is a memento of World War II, a bawdy old sea shantey that was laundered for radio presentation during the war. Jimmy Brown, who sang it, was also a memento of the World War II Lombardo band. He was one of a succession of singers who stayed with the band briefly until they were drafted. "If you announced a singer's name on the air," Guy recalled recently, "the next day he'd get a call from the draft board; so we stopped mentioning their names."

"When My Dreamboat Comes Home"

This song typified the slow treatment the band gave to songs that others played much faster. It starts with brother Lebert's soft muted trumpet solo. "His idol," Guy recalled, "was Louis Panico, who played in the old Isham Jones band. I remember when Lebert, who was only a kid, met Panico. Panico told him, 'Listen to me and to Henry Busse and King Oliver and others, and then make up your own style.'" Lebert also sings this song, written by Dave Franklin and Cliff Friend, who brought it to us on a Sunday afternoon during our rehearsal for our Bond Bread radio show. We flipped over it and recorded it three days later."

"Swingin' in a Hammock"

While the Lombardo orchestra was playing for dinner at the Roosevelt Hotel in New York in 1930, a woman named Tot Seymore danced by the bandstand and handed Guy the lead sheet of a song she had written. Guy glanced at it, passed it along to Carmen, who took a quick look and nodded. While Miss Seymore was having dinner, Boyd Bunch put together a quick arrangement of her song, "Swingin' in a Hammock," and by the time she had finished eating, the band was ready to play it for her. It became her first hit and one of the Lombardos' biggest hits in their early years in New York.

"That Everlovin' Rag"

During the early years of the Lombardo band, the brass section consisted of Lebert Lombardo on trumpet and Jim Dillon on trombone. Later, Guy heard about a musician who played a brass horn that was midway between a trumpet and trombone. His name was Dudley Fosdick and he called his instrument a Fosophone. Fosdick, who had previously played with Red Nichols' jazz band, brought a new sound to the Lombardo orchestra, and when he eventually retired, his Fosophone solo on "That Everlovin' Rag" was taken over by Walter Smith, playing mellophone.

"Boo-Hoo"

When Prohibition was repealed, Carmen Lombardo wrote an appropriate song, "Let's Drink." The band played it but nothing happened. A year later Carmen had another idea for the same melody, "Gay Paree." "It was a bomb," said Guy. Then Carmen hummed the melody to songwriter Edward Heyman, who was getting on a boat to Bermuda. "Boo-Hoo," said Heyman, and left. Carmen and John Jacob Loeb dashed out new lyrics and "Boo Hoo" was played at the Roosevelt Hotel in New York that night. It shot to No. 1 on the Hit Parade and stayed there for seventeen straight weeks.

JOHN JACOB LOEB

There are so many more personal incidents behind the hundreds of tunes which have been sold in the hundreds of millions by the band. It would take a separate book to relate them all. It somehow seems fitting that the sentimental sound of "The Sweetest Music This Side Of Heaven" blends with the sentimental side of their selections.

Friends Remember

Freddy Martin

Bandleader Freddy Martin, one of the musical greats, remembers his association with Guy Lombardo going back to the beginning of his career in the late twenties, before the thought of becoming a bandleader entered his mind.

The locale was the Music Box in Cleveland, Ohio. Freddy played the saxophone in his high school band and on the side had his own little group playing for small dances at the rate of about two dollars a man. He also had a job working after school, on weekends, and during the summer vacation for a musical instrument factory where he sold reeds, instruments and various musical appliances, made trombone oil and put new heads on drums.

In the evenings, Martin traveled to various night clubs trying to sell instruments to the musicians and his favorite stop was the Music Box. The Lombardos recognized him because he was there almost every night and they were interested when he told them he had his own group. When they received an offer to play a weekend prom, they asked him to audition for them. Freddy Martin was hired and was ecstatic. It was to be his first professional engagement, and those few nights are treasured memories. Incidentally, he never sold one single instrument. A salesman he was not.

Four or five years later after Freddy had been a sideman in many orchestras throughout the country, he again met the Lombardos in New York City where he started another band that was playing at the Bossert Hotel in Brooklyn while Guy was the musical toast at the Roosevelt Grill in Manhattan. Freddy and his wife Lillian often went dancing there and count themselves among the many who romanced along with the beautiful melodies.

When his orchestra was playing at the Waldorf Astoria,

Freddy had an offer of a five-year contract to play at the Aragon Ballroom in Chicago. Never having played a large ballroom, the idea overwhelmed him. He called Guy for his opinion and Guy said, "Listen Freddy, if it was good enough for Wayne King with his broadcasts every night, I think you should do it." He did. Guy was right.

Freddy Martin was honored when Guy, just after Carmen's death, asked him to "front" his orchestra for him for a week. Naturally, thoughts of Carmen were on everyone's mind. Freddy was glad, however, that Guy thought of him for this unforgettable experience. It made him feel close to Carmen, whom he loved and respected.

In the early days when Guy decided to add another saxophone to the orchestra, Martin was under consideration but Guy decided to hire Larry Owens, a local bandleader. If the decision had been otherwise, Freddy Martin might still be there.

E. Y. Harburg

The phone rang. A voice resonant with Broadway exuberance (not necessarily sincerity) greeted me with "Yip, you don't remember me....but I'm a great admirer of yours......" Now, this is an opening that could get me out in a blizzard to see a hanging, even tho' it was I in the noose of the rope.

The voice belonged to the buoyant Saul Richman, Broadway's cheerful cherub and manager for Guy Lombardo. I later discovered that everybody working for Guy Lombardo was blessed with the same cheerful cherub syndrome, which reflected the security of working for a man who had achieved inner peace by giving pleasure to others.

The call was to invite my collaborators, Fred Saidy, Burton Lane and me to meet with Guy Lombardo to discuss presenting Finian's Rainbow at Jones Beach the upcoming summer of '77. The maestro was a legend to us, though none of us had ever met him. We were picked up by a chauffeur in his cozy limousine and whisked off to Newark, New Jersey, to a sprawling middle class restaurant made to accommodate the population explosion of the middle aged and elderly.

This outpost of dreamland was a far cry from the far-out cries of the discotheques. It was a refuge from the wounded howls of the narcissistic young, the violent jungle drums and the psychedelic lights reflecting the fearful world of police sirens, ambulance shrieks, and dazzling floodlights of engines rushing to a fire. It was a refuge from a time of love without courtship, sex without love, fun without joy and music without melody.

The gently graying haired couples that clung to each other on the dance floor needed none of this as they floated on nostalgic rhythms of a gentler day, led by that old endearin' maestro who towered above the band with his magic baton

"Yep, Yep — Guy Lombardo and his band has always been my favorite band . . . His trumpet playing brother has always been in my mind as my first chair man in my dream band if he ever leaves the Guy . . . Over in Europe (where I'm about to make another trip real soon) they all can tell you I've always had the greatest respect for Guy and his brothers — personally as well as musically.

"I shall never forget the night Zutty and I paid the Lombardo band a visit out at the Granada in Chicago. They treated us so well I'd be there all night explaining how thrilled Zutty and I were. They introduced us, we sat in, sang, and just felt at home . . . I've never forgotten it . . . I said to myself, "My, My, here I am sitting in with my favorite band — the band we've broken our necks to get to the Ranch to hear."

Sonny Werblin and former Decca Records prexy Milton Rackmil 'clown it up' at Jones Beach.

David "Sonny" Werblin

"There were so many warm and loving moments that I have shared with Guy and Lilliebell that it is almost impossible to pick out any single one. Aside from the normal business relationship, our personal lives were very close.

"One incident that stands out in my mind is when Guy, Lilliebell, and I were out "harpooning" hammerhead sharks off Freeport on a sunny afternoon. I used quotes around the harpooning because, at that time, our harpoon consisted of a long window pole with a knife fashioned to the end of it.

"Guy and Lilliebell had a wire-haired terrier named Rowdy, who was the defendant in more lawsuits than any Watergate participant, inasmuch as he bit everyone indiscriminately. This meant nothing to Lilliebell, since it was a question of whether Guy could even cope with this beast for her affection. At any rate, as Guy picked up his harpoon and threw it into the shark-infested water, Rowdy attached himself to his wrist and Guy promptly threw him overboard only to find himself hit the water as quickly as the dog, since Lilliebell immediately pushed him overboard."

John Wilson

Guy Lombardo was consistently successful for such a long period of time that people in the last forty or fifty years have tended to assume that he had always been what he became in those later years of his half century as a top name in the entertainment world.

Consistency was his hallmark, and the consistency of his readily recognizable style, which changed in only the subtlest of ways as the years passed, was the source of both his popularity and the sarcasm that was leveled at him. Dancers and listeners alike flocked to hear the Royal Canadians because they knew what they were going to hear, current hits, old standards, and established Lombardo favorites, played in a lilting style that was so inimitable none of Guy's imitators could catch its full flavor. To his detractors, the very fact that Guy stuck to the same style year after year made him old-fashioned and corny.

And yet, by the time Guy died in 1977, almost fifty years to the day that he and his band had shot to overnight fame in Chicago, few of his followers and none of his detractors remembered that when he introduced the style that gave the Royal Canadians their identity, he was viewed as a radical by the pop music establishment and his major following was on college campuses.

Today it seems outlandish to think of Guy Lombardo as a musical radical. But in the music world of 1927, he was. Dance bands in those days played everything in a bright, staccato, herky-jerk manner that was considered to be "jazzy." The smooth, flowing lines of the Lombardo approach and the sensuous purr of his saxophone was completely at variance with what was expected of a dance band. It was so strange, so different, so "radical" that when the executives of Columbia Records first heard a recording submitted by this new band from Chicago, they were prepared to turn it down on the basis that it was impossible to dance to this music.

The fact that no one has ever had any trouble dancing to the Lombardo music was evidenced by the crowds of dancers that packed the dance floor of the Granada Cafe in Chicago where the Royal Canadians made their reputation. They went on the air from the Granada for the first time on Nov. 16, 1927. They began broadcasting at 9 p.m. in a virtually empty room. They had been scheduled to play for fifteen minutes but when their time was up, the station told them to keep on playing. They continued to broadcast, past ten o'clock, past eleven o'clock. By midnight the Cafe was filled with people who had heard the music on the air and had been drawn to it as though Guy and his musicians were Pied Pipers.

ACKNOWLEDGMENTS

Thanks to Helen Powers and Betty Meyers for their fine editorial assistance and encouragement. Special recognition to Scarlett Creech, who worked so hard against so many deadlines in designing this book and jacket, as well as in the preparation and organization of it. To Barry Kramer, Liz Lombardo, Kenny Gardner and Max Hirshfield, my deep appreciation for their photographic cooperation and help. A salute to Bob Wahls for his friendly advice and neighborly attention. I am also grateful to Robert Moses, Richard Rodgers, George Burns, the late Louis Armstrong, Phil Harris, Freddy Martin, John Wilson, David Rose, E. Y. Harburg, David (Sonny) Werblin, Gary Stevens, and Bob Hilliard for their personal reminiscences. Not to be forgotten are Bill Simon and Reader's Digest for their cooperation. Finally, thanks to the many fans of the maestro and his Royal Canadians for their encouragement, which helped so much to make this tribute to Guy Lombardo possible.

Preceding page: New Year's Eve at the Waldorf with the Royal Canadians.